A WRITER'S WORKBOOK

A WRITER'S WORKBOOK

DAILY EXERCISES FOR THE WRITING LIFE

Caroline Sharp

ST. MARTIN'S PRESS

NEW YORK

www.stmartins.com

Library of Congress Cataloging-in-Publication Data

Sharp, Caroline.
    A writer's workbook: daily exercises for the writing life /
    Caroline Sharp.
      p. cm.
    Includes bibliographical references.
    ISBN 0-312-24272-7
     1. Authorship—Handbooks, manuals, etc. 2. Authorship—
    Problems, exercises, etc. I. Title.

    PN147 .S4627 2000
    808'.02—dc21

                                  00-024761

First Edition: June 2000

10 9 8 7 6 5 4 3 2 1

*I dedicate this book with great love and thanks to
the man who makes the world safe for me—
my best friend, my husband, Jamie Curtis.*

Contents

Acknowledgments

A Writer's Workbook is a project that has been a long time in the making. Along the way, there have been many people without whose help I would have faltered and failed: I would like to thank them by name.

First and foremost, the *Workbook* never would have seen the light of day without John Hodgman, the best agent a writer could ever hope to have. He believed in this project, and saw its potential, when it was just a thirty-page prototype. His kind and wise hand guided it through the many months of hard work it took to get to publication. Whatever I needed: hand-holding, explaining, encouraging, he was up to the task and always offered 110 percent. I am indebted to him for this project and look forward to many projects to come. Onward and upward.

I owe a great vote of thanks to my editor, Marian Lizzi. I had hoped for someone who would seriously and carefully read my work: What I got was an editor who read and reread and reread each sentence, helping me to push each page into its best possible shape. Marian is a conscientious and accomplished editor. Her enthusiasm and commitment have greatly improved my best effort. I am lucky that we had the chance to work together.

When the prototype of the *Workbook* was finished, and I was without agent or publisher, I didn't know anyone in the publishing business and was at quite a loss as to what direction to pursue. Two people were very kind to me at this anxious stage: Beverly Sills and Diana Burroughs. Beverly, my surrogate mother, was both inspiring in her advice and helpful with her ideas. Diana is one of the most generous and dependable people I know; if she says she will help you, she does; if she says she'll make phone calls, she makes them; and if she makes suggestions, they are appropriate. I am indebted to both of these wonderful women for their time, energy, and initiative.

I always knew I wanted to write, but it took many years before I believed that writing could be my career. There were people along the way who believed in me, and those who did not. I want to thank them all—as each of them, in their own way, contributed to this moment. For brevity's sake, here are the key players: Marianne Grose, you were the first adult who took an interest in my writing and your kind ear and gentle encouragement came at a time in my life when it was as necessary as air. Joel Millner, you taught me more about the film business in one year than I learned in three at Columbia University. Brian Helgeland, you were my first mentor; your astounding talent is only matched by the focus, discipline, and dedication that you apply to your craft on a daily basis. You are a standard I will never equal but one to which I will spend a lifetime aspiring. Jeff Gordon, your outlining structure is one I have used and adapted to everything I write. Your sense of humor and generous encouragement of my work will not be forgotten. Rene Apel, Elizabeth Korte, Jed Cohen, Paul Welsh, Ann and Sarah Blanchard, Garrett Sadler, Jennifer Lewis, Pamela Murphy, Elizabeth Gilbert, Sharon Gitelle: You all have been the most charitable, considerate supporters of my writing over the years. A person could not ask for better readers. A gal could not hope for better friends.

Viola Brown, this *Workbook* would, quite simply, *never* have been written without your help. You gave me a room of my own in which to work, and quiet hours during which to think.

My aunt, Mary Cronson, has been a consistent champion of my work, always taking an interest, always ready to watch a first edit of a student film and always willing to read a first draft of a story. Your attention is appreciated. My cousin, Caroline Cronson, has been a regular reader, a personal advocate, and a consistent believer in me as a person and a writer. My mother-in-law, Kleanthe Curtis, and my sister-in-law, Madelon Curtis, both read the *Workbook* in its entirety in each of its many drafts. Their support, enthusiasm, and encouragement is greatly appreciated.

Jennifer Adcock, my faithful assistant. Your relentless interest in this project has helped me more than I can say. You read every word as it came off the printer, proofread every page, and typed up the bibliography. You are an integral part of this project.

Finally, my family. My dear husband, Jamie, and our two children, Margaret and Henry. Waking up every morning knowing that you three people are in the world is a blessing. Thank you for helping me to do something productive with my life.

Foreword

One fine afternoon I was sitting at home staring at a wall and decidedly not writing when I received a welcome telephone call. (When I am not writing, all telephone calls are welcome, just as when I *am* writing, all telephone calls are outrageously offensive.) This particular call was from my good friend Joe, himself a writer. As it turned out, Joe was also sitting at home that day, also staring at a wall, and also decidedly not writing.

"Let me pose a hypothetical question," he began.

"Certainly!" I settled in for a delightful episode of procrastination.

"What would you rather do?" Joe asked. "Would you rather wash all your dirty laundry, run it through the drier, fold it, put it all away in your drawers, and then take those same clean clothes *out* of your drawers, unfold them, and wash them *all over again,* or . . . would you rather spend the same amount of time writing?"

"Laundry," I replied without hesitation. "I would definitely do the laundry twice."

Joe's question brought up one of the more interesting features about writing; namely, how much we hate it. For people who make big claims about loving the written word, authors will do almost anything to avoid actually *writing* those written words. And for the aspiring writer, the work always seems especially impossible. How to begin? Where to begin? How to motivate? How to find discipline when no encouragement or incentive exists? The obstacles to becoming a writer are seldom a lack of inspiration or talent, but almost always a lack of will. It is very painful to sit down and write. It's hard work. It's not rewarding. It's not good exercise. It's not sexy. It's frankly a lousy way to spend the afternoon. After a few discouraging hours of it, almost anything can look better than a blank page. And as long as the aspiring writer continues to value dirty laundry over blank pages, very few novels will actually get written.

What Caroline Sharp has done here in *A Writer's Workbook* is to offer up the world's most generous favor to those among us who would write and could write if only we could get down to work. What she has done here is no small accomplishment. It is not easy to teach people anything about the mechanics and the mystery of writing. In fact, there is an eternal debate within the literary world as to whether people can be taught to write at all. While there is a marvelous tradition across the centuries of conservatories where students can study music, or studios where ambitious artists can develop new styles, or dance companies where young ballerinas can train under the great masters, there is no such tutorial history in the art of writing. Writers have always been completely on their own.

The idea of a writing class (or, even more revolutionary, a writing *program*) is a very new idea, unique to late twentieth-century America. I have long questioned the wisdom of spending money to take a writing class. I have always believed there are two good reasons that writers have not traditionally studied their craft in a formal environment. For one thing, as writers we don't *need* to travel to Paris to study under the great masters; printed books can bring the great masters to *us,* right into our homes, where we may work under an author's mentorship long after that author has actually died. But what's more important to understand is that writing is an inherently solitary pursuit. It is perhaps not such a good idea to get too addicted to the workshop or to the classroom or to the constant and immediate feedback of your peers. The fact is, when the time comes to produce words, it will just be you and your heartbeat alone in the room. And you'd better be ready for that room. You'd be ready for that heartbeat.

Caroline Sharp can get you ready. Her marvelous book is not a course in writing, nor does it claim to be. Caroline Sharp cannot and will not show you how to be a good writer. That is entirely up to you, dependent upon your natural gifts and the level of your commitment. Instead, Caroline Sharp shows you how to actually get down to work. And being able to work is half the struggle.

How to begin? She tells you, starting off with simple stretches to warm you up and get you to actually put your hand to the page.

Where to begin? She offers dozens of clever gimmicks to set you off and hone your skills.

How to motivate? With humorous anecdotes and the most profound empathy, she boosts your morale.

How to find discipline? Well, she will also kick your lazy butt into gear, if that's what you need.

Sharp—a preternaturally gifted storyteller, who has been down that blocked road many times herself—knows exactly how it feels to be stuck midsentence. She knows the panic, the depression, and the frustration of physically being unable to write. She's been there, and yet she has come out of it alive. Moreover, she has come out of it with tricks that will help you get out alive, as well. *A Writer's Workbook* is funny and smart and accessible, but more than anything, it is extremely valuable. This is a book for students, for professionals, for poets, for playwrights, for journalists, and for those of you who don't even dare call yourselves writers yet, except in the most secret moments of the night.

Honoré de Balzac, while arguably not the *best* authority on writer's block, being that he managed to churn out some ninety novels in his lifetime, nonetheless had the best explanation of why writer's block must be vanquished. He wrote in no uncertain terms:

> If the artist does not throw himself into his work . . . like a soldier against a fortress, without counting the cost; and if, once within the breach, he does not labor like a miner buried under a fallen roof . . . then the work remains unfinished. It perishes, is lost within the workshop, where production becomes impossible and the artist is a looker-on at his talent's suicide.

Grim projection. Nobody wants that. But it does happen. Roofs do cave in. If you are in trouble, Caroline Sharp cannot dig you out of your collapsed mine. She wouldn't even know where to *find* you in your collapsed mine, since a writer's work is always so personal. But what she does do with *A Writer's Workbook* is to toss you down a rope, a flashlight, and a helmet. Trust her. The tools she offers up in these pages are essential and will lead to many a fantastic act of self-rescue. If you are trying to dig yourself out from under writer's block, this book is a real salvation. It is a wonderful glimpse of daylight ahead.

—Elizabeth Gilbert

Introduction

The idea for this *Workbook* and the birth of my second child happened within a month of each other. It occurred to me that it was time to pick my pencil up and begin to write again. I hadn't written at all during my pregnancy—nine months of morning sickness. But now, as the baby was growing stronger and bigger every day, I recognized that familiar nagging unease: *You should write today. Why didn't you write today? Will you ever be able to write again?*

Pieces of paper floated in my dreams. My treasured fountain pens seemed to glare at me from their spot on the desk. I began to panic. Something was stuck in the machinery! Something was jammed up, blocked! The words weren't flowing; the sentences were not popping out and onto the page. No paragraphs. No stories. No writing at all . . . at all . . . at all.

It finally began to make sense as I watched the Olympic gymnastic team on television being interviewed about their hopes for gold. They talked about all that they had to do to get ready for competition. As I saw footage of the gymnasts running and stretching and tumbling, it occurred to me just how much preparation went into their every step and turn. It may seem accidental, I thought, or easy, or effortless, *but it was not.* It was all about *PREPARATION: groundwork, effort, work, toil, struggle, planning, rehearsal, organization.*

This was the deal: If I wanted to learn to play the piano, I would play scales, arpeggios, octaves. I would build up the strength in my fingers, learn to read music, study the masters, play for hours every day. If I wanted to learn to speak a language, I would enroll in a class, study the grammar and vocabulary, read newspapers and simple books in that language.

The gymnastics team worked on every single element of their

routines, breaking it all down to its component parts and rehearsing and rehearsing and rehearsing. And yet I expected to
pick up a pen, after a nine-month break, and waltz right back
into my old habits. I set the bar at an unrealistic height and was
surprised, and disappointed, not to clear it. Has this ever happened to you?

Once I realized what my problem was, the next step was devis-
ing a solution. I needed to get back into practice, back into the
daily routine of writing. I needed to exercise the muscles, the
writing muscles, the parts of my eyes and hand and brain that
would shape me back into being a writing person—a person who
writes—a WRITER. I have long believed that the greatest pitfall
of my profession is the desire *to be a writer* . . . this sets up a profile
of a PERSON, unattainable and mystic. A mirage. I don't know
who this strange person is, this *writer,* but I do know how to write.
And, perhaps, if I do the work, if I do the behavior LONG
ENOUGH, I will become the person. If I write, I will be a writer.

So I needed to set up a course, a structure of exercises and
routine assignments and lessons to do on a daily basis. Some to
develop my ear, some my eye, some to work on particular stories,
and some just to work on my ability to hear conversations in the
booth next to me at the coffee shop. All of the exercises would re-
quire daily writing. Each would take about an hour.

I developed this book for myself, but I do believe that you can
use it, too. I do believe that anyone, anyone wanting to write, can
get something from it. We all need to practice, to "exercise," even
the most successful among us; and this workbook puts in a practical, portable format the daily requirements of our craft. We
need to write, and we need to write a lot. So here's some stuff to
write about. Have fun.

How to Use This Workbook: A Few Suggestions

I know that it is often tempting just to crack open a fresh, new project and dive in, but the five minutes it will take you to read this section will pay off. Each of the thirty-two exercises is explained in detail in the hopes that it will help your writing to try them all, at least once, in the way described here. After you have tried each exercise once, you may well find certain ones that you like better or that you feel help your writing more than others. You may want to change an exercise to suit your writing needs. Go ahead. THIS BOOK IS FOR YOU!

I have tried to report the possible/potential uses of each exercise. For instance: the PICTURE THIS exercise. You will read about how to *set it up:* Tape, clip, paste, or staple a visual image to the top of these pages. *How long to spend:* Start with ten minutes and build up to thirty. And, most important, *What is the purpose of this exercise and why am I doing this rather than watching* People's Court *and drinking coffee???* That is a longer answer. You will discover the purpose. You can make this exercise work for YOU.

Each of the thirty-two exercises addresses a specific aspect of this crazy craft we call WRITING. For the most part, you will be able to "do" an exercise in half an hour. If it is at all possible, you should try to put half an hour EVERY DAY into writing a journal page as well. I know this is a lot of time—you are probably working full-time, maybe in school and working. Perhaps you have children, also demanding your time. How can I suggest that you pull yourself in even one more direction? Stretch yourself even thinner?

It is all for this one reason: You want to be a better writer. It matters to you to be able to express yourself with words, to create characters, write a story. Your journal pages are your "wake-up," your warm-up, a daily "welcome to the word." They will help to focus you, remind you of why you want to write, and—on some particularly harsh days—remind you how *to* write.

You will no doubt notice that, throughout this workbook, I have used both books and movies as examples to illustrate certain story and character techniques. This is not to say that a book and a movie are the same thing. However, in these ripping-past-you days, we don't always have the time to read as much as we would like. I use movies as references because they are a common language of these times. Just about everyone has seen *E.T.*, not everyone has read *Remembrance of Things Past*.

A WORD OF CAUTION: While you will have favorites and may even hate certain of the exercises, try to do each one at least once. I also recommend that you start a calendar page on which you keep track of your daily writing: which exercise you did, how long you spent on them, the date and time. This will give you an overview of your progress and the direction of your interests. Watch for patterns: A week full of "character pages" might tell you something about your mood, your energies, your life.

Before starting each of the exercises, read the "Workbook Suggestion" page. Then sit down; get your pencil, pen, or whatever you prefer to write with; clear off a space in front of you; glance at your watch; and get going. This is the most exciting time of your day. It's *your time.* Who knows what you will create? Who knows what you will discover along the way? This is the adventure of the blank page—the most challenging and irritating and exhilarating and inspiring part of the day—THE WRITING PART.

All right, I'll admit it. I think that being a writer is the most wonderful profession in the world. I think that writing is the most wonderful thing to do. Anything that interests you—*anything* at all—whether it is the minerals of the Grand Canyon or the Wright Brothers or sixteenth-century Carthusian monks, if it grabs your fancy, you can research it, write about it, learn about it, live it. You can walk among any people who tickle your fancy.

You can place yourself in any time, place, world, sex, height, face, income, size, age, whatever. You are bound only by the limits of your mind. You are constrained only by the weight of your pencil and the space your pad of paper takes up. Any place you want to go, you can go. It's the last great frontier. It is a limitless frontier.

No wonder so many people want to write. And yet, except for "Hello" and "I used to play the piano," I hear the phrase "I want to be a writer" more than any other. It is usually accompanied by a wistful expression and a downcast eye. It is an expression of regret usually. Why?

As I mentioned before, I believe that this is because of the immeasurable and insurmountable gap—no, chasm—between the act of writing and the event of being a writer. Anyone can write. We write lists, we write checks, we write "OUT OF ORDER" notes for the parking meter and toilet and pay phone. So what is the mystic, mythical transformation that occurs when we *become* a writer?

Here's what this one writer thinks. There are such clear-cut stages and tangible procedures for attaining many of life's professions. The Series 7 exam to be a stockbroker. The LSAT for law school. Med school to become a doctor. Belts of different colors to learn karate. A test to get your driver's license. But, as of yet, no one has come up with a solid, universal standardized test for becoming a writer. Nothing so that, at a cocktail party, you can stir your ice cubes with that cocky flair and say, "Yup, I passed it last month. *I'm a writer, for sure. Aren't you?*"

So we're all floating around in a state of confusion and insecurity, looking for publication as our only real measure of success and validation. And because so few people get published, and even fewer then go on to making any real money, are we all failures? Are none of us writers? Are we all wanna-bes?

Tricky question. I have long defined myself as a writer, before I got anything published, before I got an agent, before I made a dime. I have known I was a writer since I was twelve, maybe even before that. And how? Because *I didn't want to do anything else but write.* All I wanted to do was write, ever, always, and amen. And because I wrote every day, I got better, just a little better, every year; and I am a better writer today than I was five years ago. The story I wrote last year was preceded by the one before that, and the story I write tomorrow will lay the groundwork for the one to come next year. I'm writing as I live, writing about my living, and learning from the living and the writing and the reliving and the rewriting.

I guess that no one has the right to say anyone else isn't a writer, or isn't talented, although God knows it's tempting. I guess that we are writers if we write, if we write all the time, if we improve, and if we want to do it more than anything else. I'm not absolutely positive, but I believe that I am a writer. And, today, if you are writing and not looking back over your shoulder too often, you can be one, too.

OBSTACLE PAGES,

or . . . Reasons Why You Just Can't Write—Today

As the text for this workbook was nearing completion, and I was beginning to see the *entirety* of it, the *wholeness* of it, it became increasingly obvious that something was wrong.

The exercises were all finally coming together; the form and shape of the manuscript was gelling. But something was missing. It was a body without a heart.

I had not addressed the *emotional* side of writing, the deeply rooted, completely irrational "I Can't Do This" reasons people use to explain why they couldn't write yesterday and most likely not tomorrow and certainly not *today*. Is it fear? Anxiety? Lethargy?

What kind of "road blocks" do we put in our own paths? We think for days and weeks and years that we *want to write*. We know we need to sit down with *some form* of the pencil/paper partnership. We know that words are involved.

We do have stories we want to tell, stories that burn inside of us, messages that we desperately want to leave behind as a record that we were here. But we *don't do it*. We didn't do it yesterday, we aren't doing it now, and, unless something changes, tomorrow doesn't look good either. Every day you want to write and don't write is another notch on your tree of torture.

If any of this sounds familiar, take a look at the Obstacle Pages found throughout the book. There are seven of them and there could have been many more. They are the excuses we use. The whitewash. The doctor's note we keep on handing in for ourselves. Maybe you will be able to read one and say, "Yeah, that's me. I do that. I did it yesterday—but I'm not doing it *today*."

WARM-UPS

These are short, preparatory exercises. They'll get you in the mood to write on days when your motivation is less strong. They can also be a day's work by themselves when time is tight.

Warm-up, Stretch, and Extend

These are quick exercises, meant to take just a few minutes each. Below are listed objects/things of an abstract or intangible nature. Without spending time in preparation, write a short paragraph on each. This is simply to work on your power of description—a very helpful asset for any writer.

Describe:

1. a circle
2. a spiral staircase
3. classical music
4. the color red
5. hot soup
6. rain
7. the smell of a barbecue
8. cold weather
9. a pillow
10. a hot cup of coffee
11. the welcoming bark of a dog
12. wood/plastic/velvet/cotton
13. a bench
14. television
15. seedless grapes
16. being nauseous
17. spilling a liquid
18. kissing
19. a pencil
20. a tornado
21. white wine
22. wet tears on your face
23. a brick
24. warm socks
25. perfume
26. fire
27. the grunt of a pig
28. rock 'n' roll music
29. silk
30. iron

JUST A THOUGHT: Some books are filled with description, others are more action oriented. These differences are labeled "low concept" and "high concept," respectively, when describing a movie. For example: *Die Hard, Rambo, The Hunt for Red October,* and "Stars Wars" are examples of high-concept storytelling. There is a common misconception that time-consuming detail is unnecessary in a high-concept format.

I disagree. No matter how swiftly your characters are chasing, or being chased, your story will always benefit by a breath of description. Motion is not a substitute for motivation. Give your story depth, and your readers will go deeper into it.

One-liners: A Quick Warm-up Exercise

I graduated from college without a *clue* as to what to do next.

Perhaps you're like me—staring at the future frozen with fear and indecision, like a deer caught in the headlights of an oncoming tractor trailer. What? What is this huge unstoppable thing charging toward me? My future? You have *got* to be kidding.

Perhaps you're one of the lucky ones, sure of yourself, certain of your destiny and the best path to take toward it. Doctor, lawyer, engineer, teacher, nurse, yoga instructor, venture capitalist . . . you saw the big picture of your life at the age of twenty-two and found it exciting, challenging, *possible.*

I knew a gal in Los Angeles who told me, without a hint of irony, that she knew exactly who she was at the age of eight. This was right after I confessed to her that I had spent my entire twenties searching for some meaning in life in general and some direction in mine in specific. She stared at me as if I was a prize nutcase. I asked her if, honestly, she could say that she never questioned her function on this planet or the direction in which she was heading. She frowned at me and, too chirpy for me, admitted that she had *not changed in the past thirty years* (she was thirty). Like that was a *good thing?*

Here's my thought: We *are* here for a reason. We each have abilities, and the trick is to search them out and figure out a way to use them. Someone famous once said that the only real tragedy in life is not to use the gifts and talents that God gave us. I will not presume to guess whether or not you believe in a God, but I do believe that this saying has merit. It *is* a tragedy, too often realized, to underutilize your abilities.

As for me, it took many years and many side trips and bizarre tangents before, at the age of thirty-four, I was able to say with certainty that I wanted to write full time. I scooped ice cream. I was a retail stock broker at Bear Stearns. I worked as an agent trainee at a literary agency. All those years, I felt incomplete and unsuccessful.

Now, with hindsight, I know why it took me so long: I had to be sure of what I DIDN'T WANT to do and WASN'T ABLE to do. Only then could I face forward with conviction and say, Yes, this is who I am. This is what I do want to do. I want to write. That would be an external representation of my internal self. If I spend my life writing, it would be a good life. A fulfilled life. *Even if I am never financially successful, I will be happy with my life.*

This is a very roundabout way to say that I am a writer now, finally, and that I am glad that you have decided to try to be a better writer as well. It is hard work, but it is the best and the most rewarding work.

For the Purposes of This Exercise

Take a sheet of paper, and number the left-hand side one to twenty-five. Using your fertile imagination, or Leonard Maltin's *Movie and Video Guide,* or really any movie listing you can find, pick out twenty-five movies you have seen. Write the title down, and then describe each movie in ONE SENTENCE. It can be a long sentence, but please no Charles Dickens–type 250-word epics. If you are feeling inspired, take a second sheet and do the same for twenty-five books you have read or plays or operas you have seen.

The point of this exercise is plot. Even the most complex, convoluted story line can be synopsized. It's good practice for the day when you'll pitch your idea to a possible agent or editor (individuals with famously short attention spans). With practice, you will be able to extrapolate the main points from any story put in front of you.

Use this exercise as a drill: You are going to become expert at assessing the BIG PICTURE, and then hitting the REDUCE button. Proust's *Remembrance of Things Past* in one line? No problem. The Bible? Can do. *Lawrence of Arabia?* Piece of cake.

How would you describe *your* novel/short story/play, etc., in one line?

Stop 'n' Shop

Writing is a funny thing. Sometimes the thoughts and the plots teem out of you and you are barely able to keep up with yourself and write them down.

Sometimes you feel empty and uninspired.

This is a guarantee: If you chose to write as a career, or if you write often and prolifically but not as your primary "pay-the-bills" activity, *you will experience both feast and famine.* You will remember that amazing month when you were thirty-four and everything you put on paper was inspired and inspiring. You will also remember that horrible time last year when it was a stretch and a struggle to write your name.

Some of the exercises in this *Workbook* address the craft aspect of writing. They ask you to develop your senses, to observe the world around and inside of you, with the end hope of making you the best writer you can be.

This is not one of them. This exercise is one of the ones you can do when you feel as motivated as a bucket of mud, bogged down with life's irritating and debilitating details—but still, in some tiny, far distant part of your brain, you harbor the desire to write. It is the last thing you want to do but the first thing you feel you must do. It is your responsibility but not your pleasure.

There are easy days when there is no current against which to struggle. And then there are days like this, when it's pulling teeth to write, when you have nothing to say, not even a "don't want to write today" entry in your journal. You wonder what you ever saw in the act of writing. You would rather bowl.

For the Purposes of This Exercise

You don't need to think about the novel you're writing or the characters and plot lines you are developing. All you need to do today is show up. With a pencil.

You are in a supermarket. You are working the check-out. As hour passes hour, you ring up person after person with their baskets of food. Some people have two items, some twenty. Here comes a woman with a toddler in the shopping cart and one more in her arms. You ring up her items: diapers, apple juice, hot dogs, laundry detergent, fabric softener, Tylenol, a six-pack of Amstel Lite. What do these groups of purchases tell you about the person? A single man in his early twenties comes in every evening at six-thirty and buys a TV dinner and a liter bottle of Pepsi. What is his life like? Your imagination starts to spin stories about these customers. Is she a frozen vegetable type, or does she buy only fresh carrots and string beans and corn?

Make lists of shopping cart ingredients. Start with a relatively small group of items, say—a packet of ice cream cones, a pint of vanilla ice cream, a pint of coffee ice cream. See if you can come up with ten different combinations without repeating. Give yourself ten character profiles (e.g., woman, twenty-nine, single: e.g., man, sixty-four, widower) and write up their shopping list. Pick out a single item—say, chocolate chip cookies—and fill in around it for as many different customers as you can.

Don't be afraid to make huge assumptions about these people based on what you see them buying. You can judge these shoppers just by what is in front of you right now. It's a little bit detective, a little bit spy. What kind of person buys peanut butter and cool whip? You tell me. Why does the woman with the yellow sun hat always buy two jars of mustard, one box of saltines, and suntan lotion? Why does the old guy in the suit ask for regular milk on Monday, 2 percent milk on Wednesday, skim milk on Friday, and heavy cream on Sunday? Stranger than fiction.

This exercise is a reminder: It will remind you that you *have* an imagination, that you *can* still write on a day when your impulse is to throw out your computer, your paper and pens. Maybe today's work will never win the Nobel Prize, but it *will* help to put you back on track. You sit yourself down and start to have fun with this exercise, and before you know it thirty minutes have passed, then an hour. Your chair feels comfortable again. You don't feel like a fraud, an imposter in the House of Writing. You belong.

Pretend you are the check-out person for your favorite marketplace. Fill up at least one page with shopping lists; try for two pages. Don't forget—even this simple exercise reaches out further than it seems. As you visualize the items purchased by your customers, think about their lives, the homes they will be returning to with all this stuff, what their families are like, and who they really are. This is a trip into other people's lives by way of the most obvious (and basic) route: what they buy. Their daily essentials. What they eat and drink. We all have them.

Through the specific into the universal.

Roget's Résumé

I'm sure you're familiar with Roget's *Thesaurus*—a writer's best friend. Used the word "happy" one too many times? Look it up in the thesaurus and find twenty other ways to say how cheerful, glad, content, delighted, and pleased you are. This warm-up exercise takes a thesauruslike approach to the job market. The purpose? Think of this exercise as writing "yoga": Use it to keep your mind agile, active, alert. We all know how numb our daily lives can make us feel. Use this exercise as kindling, and your imagination as the spark. Burn up the page!

Pick a job, any job—for example, lawyer. Take a piece of paper and write the word "LAWYER" on the top. Then spend five or ten minutes writing down as many different types of lawyers you can come up with: criminal, divorce, real estate, tax, copyright, etc. Underneath each subdivision, see if you can explore further. Say, under "divorce lawyer," there could be lawyers who specialize in same-sex marriages, lawyers who focus only on custody battles, or those who live to untangle property and financial resources.

To get you started, here is a list of sixteen professions: chef, painter, doctor, singer, architect, circus performer, policeman/woman, pilot, engineer, nurse, psychiatrist/therapist, cleaner, teacher, writer, broker, child-care provider.

THE EXERCISES

These thirty-one exercises comprise the body of the writing you will do in this *Workbook*. They are grouped together by theme—not by level of difficulty. Although you will find some of the exercises easier, and perhaps more enjoyable, than others, it is recommended that you try each one at least once. Your accomplishments will be cumulative: The work you do on one exercise will influence the next one and the one after that.

OBSTACLE PAGE

What If You Don't Like Being Alone? or Writing in the Company of Strangers

This is a tricky one. At face value, it is a deal breaker. Writing is a solitary activity, right? If you want to write, don't you need to be comfortable with solitude? While there does exist such a thing as "writing by committee"—the writing staff of a television sitcom, a team of advertising copywriters—I feel safe in saying that *most* writers create alone. If this makes you feel anxious or if you are convinced that the party is going on without you every time you sit down to get some pages written, then writing might not be the profession for you.

BUT this is not a done deal. Your fate is not sealed. Consider this:

1. Children and dogs most often prefer to be in the company of others. Being alone, for them, registers as neglect and even abandonment. It feels unsafe.
2. Even though you are not four years old, and you are not a dog, you are probably still sensitive to rejection. Getting left out feels lousy. Missing stuff can hurt our feelings. It is good to feel *included.*
3. If you are passionately committed to writing, BUT you absolutely cannot bear being alone, it might be time to accept this as part of yourself and go on to "PLAN B."

PLAN B

Perhaps you could find a coffee shop or library to call your writing headquarters. You may need to have different places for different days of the week. Natalie Goldberg, in her brilliant and helpful book *Writing Down the Bones,* goes into detail on "writing in restaurants" etiquette.

You also need to consider that what is making you uncomfortable may *not* be the "alone" aspect. This may be a smoke screen, a distraction. There might be a part of the act of writing itself that your head is rejecting. If that is indeed the case, then *nothing* you do to change the externals will matter worth a damn. It's the "words-on-a-page" part you don't like.

There is also the possibility that silence is not "golden" for you. Your brain could be jangling loud because of all the QUIET in your writing place. Maybe it's TOO QUIET. Some people find it easier to concentrate when there's some low-level *sound* in the background. Chatter. Radio noise, TV, a standing fan. It's said that Mozart asked his wife to *read* to him while he composed. I understand this: It quiets the "committee" in your head and, thus freed from the babble, you can concentrate. (More on "the committee" later.) This works for puppies and people: Turn the TV on in the next room and the suggestion of companionship soothes the tension, releases the anxiety. Your sense of unease now calmed, you can start to write.

ONE LAST THOUGHT: There's no question that one person's soothing white noise is another person's fingernails on the blackboard. This is all very individual. It may take you a long time to discover the circumstances under which you will be a prolific and focused writer. Don't give up!

Step One:
Your Journal Pages

This is where it all begins.

Every day, rain or shine, good or bad—preferably raining and bad—you should sit down to your JOURNAL. This is your warm-up. This is how you stretch before the workout to follow. Your journal reveals the personality of your day. Not the "to do" list, not the "what I ate last night": Those are diary entries. Nothing wrong with diary entries, but they're not what we're going for here. We want conviction, not calories. How high is your level of tension and stress? (N.B. there is *always* tension, and there is *always* stress.) How we avoid life's difficulties is not what defines us. How we embrace them and use them *does* define us.

Journal pages are the single most important part of this *Workbook*. WHY? Because *it is hard to write*. It's hard to write every day, and it's hard to write when you don't feel like it and the kids are yelling and you have too much other stuff to do and being creative doesn't seem fun at all.

Writing will *not* always be fun. Sometimes it will seem very very much like WORK. The commitment you show to that work is directly reflected by your daily dedication: your decision to faithfully write in your journal every day. Every day. No matter what.

Throughout this *Workbook* we will be addressing the "Am I a Writer" question. I believe it comes down to this: A writer writes. That's just about it. A writer writes all the time, not because they have to, but because that is who they are, and they can't really envision their life any other way. There was no magic banner that appeared over your crib at birth saying, "Yes, this one, let's make this one's life an agonizing, lonely struggle with very little money and even less success. Let's make this one A WRITER!" You were probably meant to be a lawyer. Maybe you *are* a lawyer.

One surefire way to find out if you are a writer is this: Write every single day and see how it feels. Then try not to write every day. How does that feel?

In the very beginning, you might not be able to write for very long. See how ten minutes feels to start and work it up to half an hour. Your journal page launches your writing day: Write about how you feel, what's going on in your life, what you plan to write about, how you feel your writing is coming. Life stuff. Of course, if you are knee deep in a new, passionate love, nothing will hold you from writing about that, and so you should. Passion makes for good "journaling." Use it.

I recommend that you *do your journal page first*. Do not edit yourself, and don't try to be entertaining. If you can't shake off the feeling that someone is reading over your shoulder, or if you are concerned about confidentiality, try this: The first week of your journal pages, complete your entry for the day, and then immediately rip it up and throw it out. That way you have the experience of writing honestly and without revision, *and* your fear of someone finding and reading your work is neutralized. After a week of this, you will have internalized the experience of recording your thoughts and feelings, and hopefully, you'll be able to move forward without needing to erase your words behind you.

Whatever it takes, don't think, don't second-guess, don't edit. This exercise must come as directly as possible from your head to the page, traveling without censorship. If you get in the habit of polishing/perfecting your "first draft" as you go, you will paralyze yourself. You'll never really be able to move on to a true second draft.

This writing does not need to be interesting, or funny, for anybody. Think of it as a record book of your life, day by day. Assume that no one will ever see them. This will open you up and help the truth to appear on the page. It is hard to write without inhibition, but it feels great and it is worth striving toward.

I went to graduate school with a nice woman—let's call her Daisy. Daisy worked on the first ten pages of a screenplay the entire first year. She wrote ten pages, then rewrote them, then rewrote them, over and over and over. From September until MAY.

The hero fell in love with a doctor. Then the hero *was* a doctor and fell in love with a marine biologist. Then the hero trained dolphins and lived on an island. Then the hero and twenty other people were shipwrecked on an island. It was painful and frustrating, for ALL of us.

Why did this happen? It happened because Daisy was trying to get it PERFECT. She was trying to write the absolutely flawless first draft. And—you guessed it—it doesn't work that way. The rewrites got worse and worse as she strayed further and further from her original idea.

I once read about a famous author who wrote a thousand-page novel. She was not pleased with it but couldn't exactly figure out why. One day, after rereading the first four hundred pages, she decided that the novel really began on page 401. She threw out the first four hundred pages, and the novel hit its stride. The author realized that she had to have written those first four hundred pages *in order to have reached page 401.*

So just put it down. Put it *all* down. Look at it later. These pages are essential and private and demanding; it is hard to write every day, and it is hard to write without being "on," without performing. But you can do it, and it will be immensely rewarding. So write, without censorship, without sanction. Don't be like Daisy. Go on to page eleven.

For the Purposes of This Exercise

1. Find yourself a quiet place where you won't be disturbed.
2. Get a pad/notebook/journal. If you write on individual loose-leaf pages, you'll need a three-ring binder in which to collect them.
3. Get a pencil.

4. Using some sort of clock/watch, mark your time, and GO. Your goal is half an hour a day. More is fine, but not absolutely necessary. Use your imagination, and don't revise your work.

One last thought to you from the pen of the amazing William Faulkner:

> It is (the writer's) . . . privilege to help man endure by lifting his heart, by reminding him of the courage and honor and hope and pride and compassion and pity and sacrifice which have been the glory of his past.

Today, yes, you write for yourself. But tomorrow, tomorrow your writing may remind people of the good parts of life, and the good parts of themselves. So let's get down to it.

Reviews:
What Do You Think?

My brother and I speak at least two or three times a week. He is a passionate and devoted movie watcher: Between the local movie theaters, his video machine, his DVD player, and the regular television, he sees, on average, five movies a week. At least. He starts our conversations with vigorous endorsements—Caroline, you MUST see this, or you MUST ABSOLUTELY NEVER see that. I inevitably agree with him, not just because our tastes are similar, but his opinions are deeply felt and convincing. I listen to his reviews because they reflect how he feels and what he likes and, therefore, who he is.

This is a busy world. We race through our days, checking things off or adding things to our mental "TO DO" list. Sadly, we frequently just *sit through* the events of our lives rather than experiencing them. Our brains get set on ACHIEVE and bypass FEEL. We fear that, if we were to slow down, relax, and take in our surroundings, we might ACCIDENTALLY grind to a complete stop.

Then . . . all hell would break lose. TIME, this behemoth advancing menacingly all around us, day by day, tick by tick, would roll on by. *We must keep up* or we will be crushed, abandoned.

The odd thing is that, although our society is impatient and restless and constantly exhausted, NO ONE wants to be the first to step out for a moment and catch their breath. Resting seems too much like being *lazy*. Relaxing is for losers; naps are for the undisciplined. Right?

WRONG. This is very far from the truth. Yes, this world is fast-paced and our attention span gets shorter every year. But because of this it is ESSENTIAL that we take, no, MAKE, the time for self-reflection. Self-reflection, contemplation, meditation—these acts are behind ALL great works of art. I guarantee you that Michelangelo would have an impossible time painting the Sistine Chapel in between seeing his therapist, his trainer, working two jobs, answering his pager, his cell phone, and chatting with his agent. Creative people *need* to be still with themselves. That is the best way to know yourself and your opinions—and figuring out how to express them.

For the Purposes of This Exercise

Set aside thirty minutes or so and let's play Reviewer. If you have seen a movie, or read a book, or been to a museum or a concert—write a review expressing your evaluation. How did it make you FEEL? Did you like it/hate it? Why? How would you have done it differently? Did those people in charge hit the mark? meaning, did they say what they wanted to say, and, if not, where did it go wrong?

In order to review something, you must think about it. In order to think about one thing and think well on it, you need to develop your concentration skills. This exercise will help to develop your powers of mental focus. When you settle down to write about the movie you saw the night before, you will find that your brain takes this as a green light. Time to throw out worries, concerns, fantasies, plans. It is easy to be distracted and very hard to focus. However, the more you practice this, the better you will get. I promise.

Perhaps you will start with only ten minutes of pure concentration. This is not a bad effort. For those ten minutes, you are not thinking about your creative writing, nor about your family life, nor what's to be your next tasty snack. You will think about the movie; and each time your mind strays away, you will gently redirect it. You write and write about "X" and then—what do you know—you've been in "the zone" and forty-five minutes have flown by. You are refreshed, calm, satisfied. It's a great feeling.

AS AN ASIDE: Here are some questions you might want to work from when reviewing a movie/book/concert/ballet, etc., etc., etc. . . .

1. List the title, the creator, the producer, the year of origin.
2. List the names of key performers.
3. Did you like it? Why? If not, why?
4. In what way did it succeed?
5. In what way did it not succeed?
6. Did it touch you/affect you? How?
7. Would you recommend it/repeat your experience of it?
8. What, if anything, would you have done differently?
9. Outline the plot/program.
10. Did it remind you of anything? What?

This exercise has two benefits: First, you are practicing your observation/reporting skills. You will find you are better able to remember what you have seen and read as your recall and retention abilities improve. Second, your reviews themselves will grow into a useful library of artistic references. Your "book reports," your film reviews, etc., all these will serve you as a research tool and a record of how you spent your days. As you look back over the reviews you have written, you might be able to notice a trend: Are you seeing only *one type* of movie? Are you reading only *one type* of book? Use your reviews to show you areas in which you need to educate yourself further.

So . . . onward and upward. Watch, read, record.

Character, Character, on the Wall . . .

One thought: Character is foundation. Let's return to that later.

It's 1971. It is July, and my friends and I are on a shoplifting jag. We are encouraged by our own triumphs, and the omnipresent myth of Billy Woods, my friend Kay's brother. Billy was sixteen; we were eleven. Big difference. Billy was our hero. Aside from being cool, and blond, and not caring that he was cute beyond belief, Billy Woods *shoplifted a watermelon from the A&P supermarket.* We all agreed that that took guts. Billy had guts.

What we didn't know then was that this would be it, really, for Billy Woods and all the blond, fearless kids from childhood summers. They peaked at sixteen or seventeen. I'm sure you knew people like that: shining stars from your high school years, everything was easy for them, they were destined to rule the world. It seemed a sure thing—successful now, successful forever.

Anyway, we were shoplifting comic books and candy bars, previews to a life of crime. My dear Nanny took my sister and me for a bike ride one gray day, and when we got home, she called me over. She'd seen some contraband *Archie & Veronica, Little Dot,* and *Richie Rich* comic books in my bike basket and she wanted to know exactly where I'd gotten them.

I tried all the usual lies: I traded for them, I saved money and bought them, I borrowed them from Patty. Nanny just kept shaking her head. "Tell me the truth," she insisted. "There's a good girl."

Finally, I broke down and confessed. My heart was pounding, and I was terrified. Caught. Afterward followed all the predictable humiliations: confessing to parents, grounded for a month, returning stuff to Mr. Willoughby in his paper store, being banned from said store for remainder of summer.

Here's the thing: As the years have passed and I am now a mother myself, I finally *get* how Nanny knew that those comic books were stolen and not borrowed or traded or bought . . . SHE KNEW *ME*.

She knew me so well, as well as I know my son and daughter right now. When you really, really know someone, you see things in them and about them and for them that they cannot see themselves. Nanny probably saw a big red flashing arrow over my head that day saying, "CAROLINE IS GUILTY, CAROLINE IS GUILTY, GUILTY, GUILTY, GUILTY."

She had watched me grow, she'd watched the slow development of my abilities, she'd taught me how to brush my teeth, and she'd watched me falter with my first lie.

Remember—"Character is foundation." Let's go there now.

A house has a foundation. A solid foundation means a solid structure. A tree climbs up from its roots. A long, difficult journey really does start with one step. To understand a person, with all of their complexities and problems and promises, look to their *character*. We can live and learn and grow and change, but all this is raised up on the solid base of *character*.

For the Purposes of This Exercise

Let's look at character from three perspectives—you, people who aren't you, and fictional people.

1. For thirty minutes, write a character description of yourself. Write it so that, if I didn't know you, I might stand a good chance of picking you out of a crowd. You may want to do several different versions of this—you as a child, you as a teenager, you as a young adult. If you have a hard time writing about yourself, then this exercise is particularly important for you. Without meaning to sound dictatorial . . .

If you can't write about yourself, you're stuck.

You are the source book for your writing material. Yours are the eyes from which you first saw the world. You hold in your heart the secrets and questions and desires that will drive your ambition to write ever forward.

Don't be a stranger: Write about yourself.

2. Time to do some character studies. This exercise will work on your ability to gather facts about a person other than yourself. Start with the people closest to you: Watch them, listen to them, contemplate them. Let them be totally and completely "not you."

The more you push yourself to describe people separate and different from you, the less likely you will be to become one of those unfortunate, limited writers able only to write versions of themselves. Granted, it is tempting: As a kid, didn't you imagine yourself as the star of every fantasy story, the hero, the love interest, the champion? Well, time has passed. The act of describing others will, eventually, begin to make you observe people more closely at all times. You probably already imagine what certain people look like naked, or with two heads, or both. As a writer you need to watch people deeply. Completely. Passionately.

So . . . pick a person and write about them for thirty minutes.

3. Now . . . how about making up some people. As a writer, you have the great freedom to invent any world, any place, any time. The blank page is your ticket to the darkest reaches of your perverse imagination. However . . . if there are no PEOPLE living in these fabulous places, the visits will be short and dull. So . . . for thirty minutes, come up with a person and write about them, flesh them out, make them whole and real.

Start with the basics: name, age, sex, address, occupation. Then fill in the details. As you do more and more of these, it will become obvious to you what aspects of creating character come easily to you and what areas need work. Perhaps you're excellent at coming up with unhappy childhood details, degenerate sex lives, and the criminal heart; but writing about kind people, nice happy folk who look out for one another, that you just can't do.

Try to become aware of these areas of difficulty. It is important to write beyond your comfort zone. Doing so, pushing yourself, is hard and irritating and can be really intense. It is also brave and challenging and will make you a better writer.

Writing is about character. Character is foundation. Character is plot. Plot is story. Story is writing. Writing is you.

Picture This

Remember *Kojak?* Police television show, hip detective, bald, lollipops, "Who loves ya, baby?" It was the 1970s, golden age for tv detective shows: *Columbo, Canon, Baretta, McMillan and Wife, Starsky and Hutch,* the Jack Klugman as a forensic one, the *blind detective* one, Longstreet or Longfellow or long something. No matter your specialty, your demographic, there was a detective show fit for you and your wife, your husband, your raincoat, your bird, your horse, your dog. Your Tootsie Roll pop.

Then the public's fancy shifted, and those now out of work had to be creative and find other stuff to do. Telly Savalas, not an overnight discovery as Lieutenant Kojak, found a lot of things to keep himself busy: television movies, a singing career.

A singing career? Yes, I own a recording of Telly Savalas singing a heartfelt rendition of "If a Picture Tells a Thousand Words." It is on a compilation record, along with Capt. James T. Kirk singing "Lucy in the Sky with Diamonds." Makes you damn proud to be an American.

Kojak spoke the truth on the mean streets of New York, and, by God, he spoke the truth on that spinning disk. A picture *does* tell a thousand words. Let's think about that a moment here, and figure out how we can put it to use in your quest to be the very best writer that you can be.

It's Sunday. You visit your grandparents. Over pie and coffee, they take out a worn photograph album and—for the 650th time—you look at pictures of you as a flower in the class play about spring. You find a box of photographs and other mementos under your bed as you look for the other sneaker: Instantly you're back at camp, or college, or that summer romance, or the year you lost twenty-five pounds.

You keep photographs of a loved one who has died. They become as important to you as anything else you own. You hold the pictures, you stroke the faces and the hands, you close your eyes and listen for their voice and wait for the sound of their shoes clicking on the kitchen floor. To lose the pictures would mean to lose a piece of the person themselves. You simply cannot do that.

But let's not limit the definition of "pictures": Technically, they are not just photographs, and they certainly don't have to be taken by you or by anyone you know. Images of a crying child running down a street in Vietnam. Soldiers in battle. A flooded town. An earthquake in Mexico City. Trees piled like matchsticks after Mount Saint Helens erupted. Students lying down before tanks in Tiananmen Square.

There are images beyond family photographs and news/ reportage. We record things visually just as much as we do verbally. The cave paintings in Spain and France. The great painters of the Renaissance. The Impressionists. The Futurists. The Outsider Artists. The senior ladies in the YMCA watercolor class in Natchez, Louisiana, Thursdays at 2:30 P.M. Any city kid with a box of chalk and a sidewalk.

So how did we get from Kojak crooning to kids and chalk? The connection is this: A visual image can stimulate our memories, possibilities, alternative realities. I see a picture of a banana tree and I think—Where do banana trees grow? Who lives there? Who planted it? Who picks the bananas? Did they get put in crates and shipped somewhere? Could I climb up a banana tree and get me a banana if I was really hungry? I remember a silly piece of trivia and wonder if it is really true: If you're in a jungle, look at what the monkeys are eating. Chances are, you can eat that same stuff, too, as monkey and human digestion parts are quite similar. I think about different types of monkeys. I think about Lucy, the oldest skull found in the world, dug up by Dr. Leaky in the Olduvai Gorge in East Africa. I think about archaeology, slow slow digs in hot places to find ancient bones.

From bananas to bones. With one memory, one spark, the imagination can be set on fire.

For the Purposes of This Exercise

Find a visual image that makes you *feel*. Tape, staple, glue, paper clip, whatever, this image to the top of a piece of paper. Write, for thirty minutes, about what's going on. Tell a story. Is it a picture of two kids on a beach?

- Who are they?
- Where are they?
- Why are they there?
- To whom do they belong?
- What are they doing right then and why?
- What will they be doing later?

This is just the barest of suggestions. The Kodak Company manages to fit a lifetime into a thirty-second commercial; you can create a universe in thirty minutes.

Think about some familiar images from our culture and try to concoct a narrative from them. What was the Mona Lisa *really* smiling about? Tell a story. Let your imagination fly. Maybe you'll write about an old high school yearbook photograph. Perhaps you have some brochures lying around: Grab one and work from the photograph on the front. Is it Saint Jude's Children's Research Hospital? Is it for Rogaine, growing hair back, or Paxil for people suffering from depression, or for a trip to Yellowstone National Park with the Massachusetts Audubon Society? We are surrounded by photographs and drawn images all day—let's put them to work for us.

Whatever you pick, you will be using your ability to pull a *story* from a frozen, static moment—kind of like a baker pulls a hot tasty baguette from a shapeless lump of dough. This is a particularly important exercise. You might think that your stories exist only as vehicles for your pleasure or as exorcisms of your own private demons. This is only partially true. I believe that the instant your characters and their destinies take shape on a page, they *have life*. They exist. And it is entirely *up to you* to make that world a *valid place*.

IMPORTANT POINT: This is not to say that your fictional world is obliged to be a rational, realistic world. If that were a requisite for literature, then Alice would never have dropped down the White Rabbit's hole. The computer HAL in *2001: A Space Odyssey* would never have had his chilling conversations. Superman would not have . . . blah, blah, blah, you get the idea. Their worlds were TRUE TO THEM.

Their worlds were (this is important) *true to them.*

The writers who gave us Stuart Little, Mothra, Scarlett O'Hara, Humpty Dumpty, Benji, the Wicked Witch of the West, and young Romeo and his girl Ms. J. ALL believed that their characters *lived* and gave them a world *in which to live.* That is what fleshed them out. That is how they jumped from TWO–dimensional flat-on-the-page to THREE-dimensional flesh-and-feelings.

SO . . . find a picture of something and write about it. Make up a story of what's going on in that moment in that world right then. Fill in with as much detail as you can. Was it cold? Can you hear music? Are the people hungry? This is a good opportunity to go way out there detail-wise: Whereas it is usually better to hold back and NOT overuse adjectives, let'er rip here. Is the air sweet, tender, spicy, slaphappy, angry, slippery? Try them all out and see how it feels. Does the child cry loudly, bellow like a bull, sing like a whale . . . or mew like a cow . . . or a bat? No rules. No Strunk and White police. Just do a Nike.

A LAST THOUGHT: The amazing Anne Lamott, author of *Bird by Bird,* an essential book filled with excellent writing advice, reminds us that we need never be overwhelmed when confronted with a big or complicated writing project. All we need to do, in the next sentence and the sentence after that, is to describe what is right in front of us. As Ms. Lamott explains, imagine yourself looking at a one-inch-square picture frame. Imagine the whole world broken down into billions of one-inch-square picture frames. You take one at a time and describe it. The BIG picture can be overwhelming. A one-inch picture tends not to be.

One step at a time. One piece of fabric sewn to another and

another and then—you have a finished quilt. Grains of sand piling up for thousands of years, finally making up a whole beach. A huge department store built one brick, one brick, one brick. The Brooklyn Bridge. The Great Wall of China. The pyramids.

Your next story: One word. One word. One word.

Finish the Thought

This exercise was one of the first five. In 1996, I had a flash idea: what about a book full of practical, daily projects for writers to help them to develop their writing skills. I spent a year thinking about it and a year putting together a "prototype." Then, by the grace of God and the kindness of a friend and fellow writer, an agent came into my life and looked at the *Workbook* prototype. At that time there were only SIX exercises:

1. journal pages
2. picture this
3. finish the thought
4. character pages
5. reviews
6. conversation observation

There were also six Obstacle pages, two Learn-a-Word pages, and four introductory sections explaining how the *Workbook*... worked. Over the past year the *Workbook* has expanded a great deal, but—and I am happy with this—the original six stayed on board.

Two women sit at a coffee shop in a busy city. One is amazingly beautiful; the other is not. The looker is agitated, distraught. She picks at her food, lights up cigarette after cigarette. She finally looks the other woman square and cold right in the face and says, "I want you to leave him alone."

What does she mean? Ten different writers would give ten different spins on this introduction. What happens NEXT? Is one a mother, another a lover? Are they talking about a husband, child, dog, employer, parent, grandfather, the president of the United

States? Who is "him" and what does "him" have to be left alone from?

This exercise will help you to develop your imagination and should open some avenues down which you may not already have ventured. It is important to try new things in your writing. You are in charge. It *is* safe. Try writing about powerful emotions, powerful situations. Try writing about food. About an old woman dying alone. A town turning on its weakest member. A man jumping into icy water after a plane crash to save a woman surrounded by jet fuel and freezing water.

Write about a child hating a parent or a nun leaving the convent or a journalist conflicted by her morals and the desire to publish a lead story. Practice, practice, practice. Stretch your voice. Assert your talent and *speak loudly* because this is a short time we have here, to be alive, here and now, with this pen and this piece of paper.

This day matters and this word matters and your story matters.

For the Purposes of This Exercise

This is not a one-day deal. This exercise will take at least two days, but it should not take much longer than five:

1. Write a setup. This should be a five- to ten-sentence paragraph in which you establish the characters involved and their drama. Leave as much to the imagination as possible. For instance, rather than:

> She held the object in her hands for the hundredth time. She felt its weight. She remembered when she and Rupert bought it at the Reject China Shop in London. That was right after lunch. It was raining.

Way too much detail. Why not try this as a setup:

> She held the object in her hands.

And let the rest ride.

When writing your setups, try to be as ambiguous as possible, about sex, age, time of day, time of the year, the year itself. Resist the temptation to explain; that will come later.

2. For thirty minutes . . . NOW it's time to elaborate. Reveal one way for the tale to be told.

3. Next—for the pure writing practice it will entail—DO IT AGAIN. For another thirty minutes, on another day, imagine a different resolution. Change as much as possible.

My recommendation is to write three versions of each scenario. This will not be easy. It will often be aggravating and frustrating. But you can do it, and in the act of working through the problems and complications that arise, you will become a better writer.

This exercise will help you with six specific aspects of your writing craft:

1. Imagination
2. Courage
3. Curiosity
4. Character
5. Persistence
6. Variety (coming up with different plots)

Maybe you're strong in one area and a bit rough and shy in another. Maybe plots come to you easily. Maybe they come to you so fast that you have to write them down on napkins and menus and your arm and someone else's arm or you'll lose them, BUT you only have the patience to try just one possible plot per story. If it doesn't fit, or if it could be better, you give up. Maybe you are a fearless writer, boldly going everywhere . . . BUT you find yourself only able to write one type of character over and over.

This exercise can open up new territories. As always, if you have the desire and the courage to look at your writing, objectively, there is always room for improvement. If you write every day, you will get better.

    Finish the thought?

           Finish the sentence?

                Finish the story?

                        Finish the novel.

Conversation Observation

Are you curious?

Do you walk closely behind people, listening to their conversations? Do you linger outside other people's homes, sometimes at night so that their rooms are lit up with that warm yellow light, looking in at their stuff and pretending then, just for a moment, that you belong there, too?

Have you ever listened in on someone else's telephone conversation? Read someone else's mail? Would you admit it if you had?

I am not advocating violating other people's privacy or property. Let's be very clear about that. However, being curious about other people and their dramas *is* a natural by-product of a lifetime spent as a writer: After all, how could you observe people and notice people and chronicle people's lives and the dramas and the adventures without having a lustful interest in them?

How close can you get before boundaries are crossed and confidentiality is breached? Start by looking at your own life and imagine someone studying YOU. Doesn't feel good, does it? No one likes to feel like a zoo display. Learning how to notice without being nosy is the delicate mission of the writer. You need to study people, listen to people, watch them, observe them, scrutinize their behavior. Gather facts about real people living real lives in real places. And you need to do this without being intrusive.

Please note that not every character you create has to, or will, be based on an authentic person. Every character will have *some* specific, real trait(s) from your observations of the world around you. There are characters in you waiting to be written, characters that only YOU can write because only you can really know them and understand them. In someone else's hand, they would not come to life.

And that character has things to SAY.

For the Purposes of This Exercise

Let's work on writing dialogue. How do people really talk? Not the perfect, neatly finished, grammatically correct way of some "literature." People speak in half-sentences. We use our hands and facial expressions and other body parts. We speak with our eyes. How do you put that on the page?

In order to write convincing, honest, satisfying dialogue, it is important and necessary to listen, listen, listen.

Your readers can't see your world. They can only read it and imagine it. It is therefore up to you to notice what's around you, practice over and over just listening and writing down what you hear. If you can get outside of yourself long enough to observe and record how *other people* speak and act, then chances are that you will eventually be able to WRITE about those *other people,* and that is the greatest thing of all. To write about people OTHER THAN OURSELVES.

But, you protest, unless I'm writing an autobiography, aren't I always writing about people other than myself?

No.

Listen. Observe. Reflect. Record.

Listen. Observe. Reflect. Record.

That's enough to keep you busy for a lifetime.

Every time you sit in a coffee shop or on a bus or under a plastic potted palm tree at the local mall, pen and pad in hand, squinting and peering around you, you're becoming a better writer. Every time you study the notes you've taken and compare them to lines of dialogue you've already written and then use them to breathe life into your dialogue, you're becoming a better writer.

This exercise requires that you spend some time in public places, places where there are other people around talking. Look around, listen, open up your notebook and write down, as fast as you can, what you hear.

Listen to voices dissimilar to your own. If you are a man, listen to women. Vice-versa. Old/young, large/small, single/married. Open up your mind and fill it with inspiration.

I recommend you do this exercise at least two or three times. In each instance, listen for half an hour to an hour, then go back to your writing place and transcribe what you got into readable notes.

This is not private detective time. You are not listening for *scandal* but for *school.* Educate yourself in the ways of social linguistics by using your most useful tool: a listening ear.

You just never know when a scrap of something you hear will be the start of the greatest character you will ever write.

OBSTACLE PAGE

Fear of Failure/Fear of Success, or "Fish of the Day"

A therapist once told me that we all have a "template" in our head on which is encoded a detailed description of who we are. It's like the hard drive of your personality computer. It knows what we like and don't like, what we want and don't want, what we will and won't do. As you go through your life, you subconsciously refer back to your "template," gauging whether all is in sync. If it is, we feel like *ourselves*. We feel *normal*.

However . . . we all know what it feels like when things go awry. Something *happens*. Things change. For some people it may be as simple as a new pair of shoes, and their usual pattern of behavior is shaken up. For other, less rigid people, it may take a major life change for them to feel rattled.

So something comes along and throws a monkey wrench in our predictable schedules. The world looks very different, it *feels*, very different. As the elements that define us shift and change, we feel less sure of *who we are*.

Fear of Failure/Fear of Success is largely a factor of revising our templates: I know who I am as "ME," but I don't know who I am as "ME DOING THAT."

Even if you truly want to succeed, there will still be feelings of uncertainty as you think about the road ahead. What will happen? Will I do okay? Will I like it? What if the path ahead holds potential failure, pain, or loss?

It can seem to make sense to cling to the known. We get accustomed to how things feel. Even discomfort can eventually feel comfortable. Now, here's the astonishing part about being human: People sometimes STAY in situations that are painful, both emotionally and physically, and accept a negative set of circumstances as their destiny, rather than make the decision to bail and brave the unknown. After all, the unknown is without reference. It is unfamiliar and scary. We pass this insidious message on to our children:

CARPE DIEM means "FISH OF THE DAY."

I don't mean to oversimplify what can be a crippling crisis. Sometimes talking to a good therapist is necessary to straighten out your old childhood baggage and begin to work on your new adult baggage. But sometimes it *is* just as basic as taking off the blindfold. We all stumble around, fall down, fail, screw up. The world *is* a scary place for everyone. Why *not* try your best? Why shouldn't it be *you* that claims the prize? Are you willing to try?

Fear of failure can be an aspect of pride; "I'm not going to risk failing." "I don't fail at things." If you never *try*, you will have a built-in excuse:

- Of course I failed the history test. I didn't study for it.
- Of course my books aren't published. I never submit them.

Twelve-Step programs suggest taking "BABY STEPS," and I believe that this applies to writing as well. Set realistic, short-term goals. *Finish* your stories. Let other people read your work. Take writing classes. Join a writing group. Participate. WHY NOT?

I believe that the only failure is not to try.

There is something to be gained from every experience, yes, even the worst *worst* most awful. It can all go into your next story. Even the falling-on-your-ass stuff.

ONE ADDITIONAL THOUGHT: FEAR OF FAILURE seems mostly to be about avoiding what we anticipate will be *too painful* for us to handle. FEAR OF SUCCESS seems, more often, to be about rethinking a negative self-image of ourselves. We will have a hard time wearing the winner's suit if we continue shopping in the loser's store.

Emulating Ernest

What does it mean to LEARN to write? Not, obviously, the physical act of ABCs and holding a stubby pencil, but the lesson-without-end mastery of the craft of storytelling? How long does it take to find our writer's voice?

How long is a road? As long as it needs to be.

Having said this, there can come a time in a writer's development when imitation becomes more than the most sincere form of flattery: It overtakes our own voice and becomes impersonation. We study the work of other writers so closely that the appropriation of their style can seem to be a natural evolution. Appropriate? Borrow? Copy? Mimic? Plagiarize? These waters can be easily muddied by semantics.

My brother—a truly gifted writer in his own right—went through a phase when his short stories were close copies of the Nick Adams stories by Hemingway. I went through a Gertrude Stein phase that now, in retrospect, is beyond embarrassing. This is not to suggest that my brother and I were faking, or forging—on *purpose*. We were not. We were trying out different voices, voices of writers we respected. Writers we wanted to be like.

Musicians are familiar with the concept of copying form. If a musician wants to write a sonata, or a nocturne, or be bold and try for a symphony, they have an established model to follow. It's not a case of plagiarism—not unless they copy the actual music written by someone else and try to pass it off as their own—as much as it is honoring an established, authentic construct. Learning these musical archetypes is part of the legacy of musical history, a tradition, as necessary as it is for a writer to learn noun, verb, adverb, and adjective.

If a musician composes in the style of Mozart, or if a painter paints in the style of Picasso, or if you write a poem in the style of Sharon Olds, are you doing a *bad thing*? Are you copying? Are you stealing?

This bears commenting on. In the lengthy process of studying a craft and developing a personal style, an artist looks back on those who have come before, those who have paved the way. We are influenced, inspired, and motivated by the work of others. It is natural, I believe, to emulate those we look up to. We try on their technique, like trying on a beautiful coat. Here's the thing: You must eventually take the coat *off*. It IS all right to practice and evolve and explore and mature as an artist by borrowing the voices and styles of others. It IS NOT all right to pretend to be someone else and to use their style on a permanent basis. It IS NOT all right to try and pass off someone else's work as your own. That *is* plagiarism, and that is not okay.

For the Purposes of This Exercise

As you read the works of the masters, the classics, you will probably get the desire to emulate their style. You may want to try to write a short story in the style of John Cheever, Truman Capote, Italo Calvino, F. Scott Fitzgerald, Alice Walker, Herman Melville, Anton Chekov, Edgar Allan Poe, Grace Paley—any master author you admire.

You may want to try and write a poem in the style of T. S. Eliot, Robert Frost, Langston Hughes, Wallace Stevens, Sharon Olds, William Carlos Williams, Pablo Neruda, James Merrill, Emily Dickinson, Gerard Manley Hopkins, Alfred Lord Tennyson.

You may want to try writing a play, or a scene, or an act of a play in the style of Edward Albee, Tom Stoppard, Shakespeare, David Mamet, Ibsen, Strinberg, August Wilson, Neil Simon, William Finn, A. R. Gurney, Terrence McNally, Robert Schenkkan.

Who's to say what parable or poem or plot will spark your inspiration? Who among us can say with certainty what it will take to set off the ALARM inside you and wake up your "muse"? The only way to tell is to go fishing. Cast out the net, wide as need be, pull in the books, dry them off, and start reading.

This exercise will reflect a little of what is in your personal library—a library made up of everything you've read and learned from and loved. Some of the books you read will affect you enough to make you want to emulate the author. You want to try out their particular, distinctive style. You want to write like them, not forever, but for right now.

As you spend time writing in the style of other writers, try to come up with a premise/plot of your own, from your time and your life: For instance, if it *is* Hemingway you're tackling, it is not necessary to set your writing in Paris in the 1920s. Let's imagine what Hemingway would sound like *today*, watching the Super Bowl, or admiring a beautiful woman serving café latte in his neighborhood Starbuck's, or trying to buy a book from AMAZON.COM. Fish out of water? Big fish, Big pond?

Your pond, their fish.

Your "Idea Book": A Lifetime Commitment

In 1987, I met someone who changed me, no—who *educated* me. She was, and still is, an artist. A painter. She lived her life as an external and active expression of her talent: Being an artist wasn't what she *did*, it was who she *was*. Everything she did, every day she lived, she moved further forward as a creative person. She lived to paint, and she painted to live.

I speak in the past tense not because she has died, but sadly because we are no longer in each other's lives. Even though I don't see her or speak to her anymore, there are many ways in which she is an active and vital presence in my life. One of those ways I am about to pass on to you.

Our friendship gelled quickly, because—aside from having a similar appreciation for good coffee and movies and travel and museums and restaurants and cute guys—we found in each other a travel buddy for life's deeper issues. We were soul mates. We could tell each other anything. We walked and talked about the directions we saw our lives taking, the problems we faced, the sorrows and burdens we carried. She accepted me unconditionally.

It was a wonderful feeling. When I was with her, I knew that I was with someone who saw the best of me and judged my lesser qualities to be unimportant. Because she thought so well of me, I thought better of myself. We grew in each other's estimation. She took me seriously as a writer. A few years into our friendship, we decided to spend the summer together in a makeshift "artist's colony." With a third female friend, a talented writer from California, we set up shop on Cape Cod in June of 1992. We met for coffee in the morning, went our separate ways for the day, and met again in the evening to talk about the day's progress. Once a week we got together for a "show-and-tell": my Californian friend and I would read drafts of our work, and my painter friend would show us the canvas on which she was working. It was a productive, peaceful, memorable summer.

One afternoon early in our second week, I wandered out to the garage in which my friend was painting. She was working on a series of small sketches as preparation for a large canvas. I sat and watched her for a while. She referred to a good-sized notebook two or three times, leafing through it and looking at several different pages. I asked her what the notebook was, and she told me that it was her IDEA BOOK.

Here's how it worked for her. She was a predominantly visual person, and she collected in her Idea Book pictures and photographs and designs, things that made it past that first "filter out" garbage barrier we all have in our mind. She might look at a coffee shop menu and be struck by the typeface or the color of a piece of Turkish money or a postcard or a leaf. Whatever she saw that inspired or roused her or that she thought might be of use for a future painting or that she just liked to look at could make it into her Idea Book.

Not every entry was a visual token. Sometimes she wrote notes. Sometimes she drew a diagram or a vignette of something she saw that she didn't want to forget. It was her book, *and there were no rules.* She told me she filled up about one book a year. I greatly enjoyed looking through her book. It inspired me to start one of my own.

My first Idea Book lasted almost four years. I bought a large three-ring binder, covered by a plastic, zippered case. It has pockets on the sides, and holds about 250 pages. It's *big*. I put in subject dividers: daily pages, specific story notes, ideas for screenplays, ideas for poems, ideas for short stories, ideas for novels, notes from books I read, notes from movies/TV shows I watched. Some entries are index cards stapled to a piece of paper, some entries are typed, some scribbled on scraps of blank paper. There are some bits of paper napkins or strips torn from theater programs. It took awhile for me to smarten up and start carrying small index cards at all times. Slow learner.

Here's the scoop: Not all of your ideas will come to you when you're sitting down at your desk. However, whenever they come, you must get in the habit of recording them—*immediately*. No matter what you may tell yourself about writing the idea down later, the chances are that you will forget—and hate yourself for it. Write it down on whatever is available. So what if people think you are a reporter. You *are,* sort of.

Your Idea Book has another purpose. Some things will come your way and give you a jolt. Or a nudge. These things should be put down, too: a sentence that you overhear, an event you observe, an interaction you experience. *You never know when something you witness will find its way into your work.*

That needs repeating.

You really never know when today's stranger will become the leading character of your next story. Once I saw a letter fall out of a mail carrier's sack and POW. My twisted imagination jumped into a short story about a man who steals one piece of mail a day for twenty-five years and devotes his life—and his apartment—to sorting and storing them. Who would have thought? It can, and will, happen to you.

Your Idea Book will be a repository. Anything that stirs your imagination can be stored there; if not in its original form (you won't be able to put a pony in your Idea Book, but you certainly can fit in a photograph or a sketch or a description), then certainly in summary. This is not your journal. You are not writing down your feelings and experiences. This is a coded scrapbook—each entry stimulates a part of your brain, and only you know the pathway back to the initial experience.

My painter friend referred back to hers on a daily basis. I can't predict how often you will use yours, but I can guarantee that, as time passes, you will get great pleasure and reassurance knowing it exists. Your next story is *there,* waiting for you.

I recommend you start an Idea Book, if in fact you don't already have one. Yours will suit your lifestyle and habits. It may or may not take the form of a notebook or a three-ring binder or a scrapbook. You may use a shoe box. Or a garbage bag (dangerous . . .). Whatever form it takes, it is yours, and it contains your inspirations and ideas and samples of the things that influence and affect you. I believe there is merit in the act of recording the phenomenon of our lives.

Oh, well, let's be honest. It's more than merit. I believe it is imperative to record our lives. Without curiosity, without the ability to look with wonder and marvel at the ordinary, without the desire to write things down because they interest us, then, well, then I guess we would not be writers.

And there is *nothing* better than being a writer.

Don't give up the fight.

To Outline or Not to Outline?

There are as many different reasons to write as there are writers. I could not *begin* to list the "why" people write, but there are some fairly universal "how's." Writing usually involves some combination of the pen-and-paper team. Being alone is a frequent ingredient. And it helps to have *some idea of what you want to say.*

Let's say you wake up with a fantastic idea: Retell the Wright Brothers' story, but instead of Orville and Wilbur being people, have them be aardvarks. Why not? Wilbur and Orville, the Aardvark Brothers, invent the first airplane, in between eating bugs and making sweet little paw prints. You think this inspiration over while having your morning coffee. By 11:00 A.M. you're sold; as you eat lunch, the Aardvark Brothers are already well on their way to Kitty Hawk.

What is the next step? Well, for some, it's time to dive into a first draft. These gung-ho, confident folks waste no time—they choose to make mistakes along the way and let the story tell itself. Although this works for some, I cannot recommend it LESS.

Let me explain. Imagine that you are going on a trip with your best friend. She comes to pick you up, and as you clamber into the car, you pester her to drop the suspense and tell you where you're going. She smiles and confesses that she has no idea. She thought it would be fun just to set out and let the road take you. No set destination, no limiting itinerary.

Does this sound like fun? After about twenty-four hours of meandering, you are at each other's throats and the trip is summarily terminated. WHY?

Because having a destination gives the trip a purpose. Each day you set out with a deliberate mission. Your trip is fulfilling a plan, and there is a reason for spending the precious minutes of your life doing this. No matter how crazy your trip might seem, to you it has a point. Without that, it is too easy to drift, slide away, get lost.

So a trip needs an itinerary, and a story needs an outline. Some type of outline. You know novels that seem to be free-floating, stream-of-consciousness-type things, but you can bet that behind every page and plot point is a well-planned motivation.

I have heard writers say that they don't like to keep to an outline because it limits them and their inspiration. I believe that this is an excuse. NEWS FLASH: Your outline is not registered with the FBI. You can change it whenever you, as the writer, see fit. The outline is not meant to restrict. An outline does not weaken the connection between yourself and your story. An outline does not impede or inhibit your spontaneity. To the contrary, an outline *frees* you. How?

1. It helps you to specify the overall direction of your story.
2. It gives you an overview of Acts 1, 2, and 3, etc. . . .
3. It points out if one of the acts is under/overdeveloped.
4. It shows you the strengths and weaknesses of your characters.
5. It reminds you, when your resolve gets weak, *why you needed to write this story in the first place.*

For the Purposes of This Exercise

First, pick a movie, book, or play that you know well, say, *Gone With the Wind*. To the best of your ability, write an outline for this story. First, how would you describe *Gone With the Wind* in one line? In three lines? Delineate the acts, and decide whether there are two, three, or more. Describe the main characters: where and when they come into the story, what is their main purpose. List the key plot points as they happen.

After you have done this for at least ten different stories, I recommend that you turn to your own ideas. On a piece of paper, write the title of your story then a one-line synopsis. Underneath that, write a three-line description.

Then begin your outline: What happens in Part One? Part Two? Part Three? Who is the antagonist, the protagonist, who are the people who live in your world? Do you know how many chapters your book will have? Why are you writing it? What do you want to say? By the last line of your book, will you have said it?

Remember fifth grade: Tell them what you're going to tell them, tell them, and then tell them that you told them. Your outline today is quite similar to your childhood essay on shrimp farming—you need a beginning, middle, and an end. You need to highlight the important bits and be clear, concise, and specific.

It is said that F. Scott Fitzgerald outlined his novels using a big bulletin board and many hundreds of index cards—each containing a small detail of the story. He moved these around until the mosaic of notes formed the picture of a complete novel. You may need to try several different outlining techniques until the most productive and comfortable one establishes itself. Remember: The outline is a tool. It's a means to an end, not the end itself. Don't get stuck in "outline rut," trying so hard to perfect the trees that you lose sight of the forest.

Have fun working on your outlines. Remember, if you know the last line of your story, it will wave and beckon in your mind, tugging and pushing your story along to meet it. You'll have a destination and a purpose. Your readers will thank you for your decisiveness, and your story will positively radiate inner energy and vigor. WRITE ME, WRITE ME, WRITE ME.

So get to work.

Where Have You Gone?

This is the sister exercise for *"Don't Know Much Geography . . . But I Should!"* which comes next. Like jigsaw puzzle pieces, these twin exercises fit together, complement each other, build upon one another. This one considers the places you have visited or lived in or even just passed through, places with which you have a personal, subjective experience.

I don't know if you have ever read a screenplay. I know that I had *not* before I went ahead and *wrote* my first tragically awful screenplay, *The Winner.* If you have ever even so much as turned to page one of an authentic screenplay, a simple simple simple act that I decided was unnecessary before launching into a 160-page first draft of my first screenplay, you would see that each scene is headed by three concise pieces of information. For example:

> INT./DAY/ROBIN'S NEST
> — or —
> EXT./NIGHT/BACK DOOR OF THE VATICAN

A genuine, legitimate, bona fide, accurately composed screenplay can be a thing of beauty. *The Winner* could never be a thing of beauty, because screenplays that begin—*A WARM SUMMER DAY/A HOUSE FROM YOUR CHILDHOOD/ABOUT 4:00 P.M.*—are doomed.

As you can see, establishing your location gets the story started. It is the first fact you learn when reading a screenplay, and it is often the first fact you learn in a story. For example:

"The Country of the Pointed Firs" by Sarah Orne Jewett. "There was something about the coast town of Dunnet which made it seem more attractive than other maritime villages of Eastern Maine."

Cold Mountain by Charles Frazier. ". . . so he came to yet one more day in the hospital ward. He . . . looked across the foot of his bed to an open triple-hung window. Ordinarily he could see to the red road and the oak tree and the low brick wall."

Invisible Cities by Italo Calvino. ". . . . leaving there and proceeding for three days toward the east, you reach Diomira, a city with sixty silver domes, bronze statues of all the gods, streets paved with lead, a crystal theater, a golden cock that crows each morning on a tower."

My Ántonia by Willa Cather. "I first heard of Ántonia on what seemed to me an interminable journey across the great midland plain of North America . . . my Virginia relatives were sending me out to my grandparents, who lived in Nebraska."

Fathers and Sons by Ivan Turgenev. ". . . His name was Nikolai Kirsanov. He had twelve miles from the posting station, a fine property of two hundred souls or, as he expressed it—since he had arranged the division of his land with the peasants, and had started a 'farm'—of nearly five thousand acres."

In truth, I've included these here for two reasons: They are examples of location being used by the masters in establishing the setting of a story, and they are also just plain wonderful to read. As a writer, it is essential to read. This sounds so amazingly obvious, and yet you would be shocked by the extent to which some writers *do not read.* True, true, true.

For the Purposes of This Exercise

This is not a one-shot deal. This exercise will take you many days to complete. Don't rush!

1. On a nice, clean, lined piece of paper, write down all the addresses of all the places where you have lived. Let's set a six-month minimum requirement. If you lived somewhere for the first four years of your life, but you have absolutely no recollection of this place, you can leave it out.

Then, one by one, spend thirty minutes describing each place. Go into some detail with each. If you can, sketch a map of your room and any other rooms you can remember. Describe your home and then the surrounding yard or sidewalks or streets or fields or beaches. . . . It will all, of course, depend on *where* you lived. Describe the interior, then the exterior.

Keep going out farther and farther in wider and wider circles. For example: Let's say you lived in Boston. You lived on Commonwealth Avenue, No. 33. Describe your one-bedroom apartment and the tiny kitchen and the tiny bathroom. The closet. The bathroom and its constantly dripping faucet. The carpet and the ceiling and the curtains and the fridge and the coffeepot and your bed. Go into as much detail as you can. Then go outside. The street. The neighborhood. The town. Any surrounding towns you visited or got to know. Then how about the state of Massachusetts?

2. After you have described all your homes, let's go to your vacations. Make a list of places you have visited on your travels. Divide the list up into three categories: childhood, young adult, adult. Again, one by one, go into as much detail as you can about the places you have visited. Did you have a romance there? Describe the sights, scents, colors, sounds. The more stuff you dredge up and put down on paper, the more you will be able to use in your stories. This is all fertile ground.

If you visited a place more than once, don't write off the repeat visits as duplications. Each stay could have created very different memories. In these cases, list the PLACE and then each of the dates you were there separately. Then try to research each individual trip using photographs, diary entries, letters you may have written, people you were there with. Use your resources.

3. Make a list of places you have been to, either for a school trip, field trip, or for work. Although this may seem to be less exciting, it is very practical and useful. Chances are, the characters you write will not always be on vacation. They will not always be on a cruise or in the south of France or Disneyland or Jamaica. They will often be at work and they could live in Dallas or Raleigh or

Oklahoma City. So don't short shrift your work trips. The character you are writing about might be a student: a fifth grader on a trip to the zoo, or a college student spending a semester abroad. The details you observe about every city you have spent time in will provide honest and colorful and interesting features for your writing.

REMEMBER: You don't need to be imaginative here. This stuff is all true. It all happened to you. Just write honestly and with specific facts and observations. Describe places you know, places you have a connection to, places where you have left part of yourself.

Don't Know Much Geography . . . But I Should!

I like maps.

I like everything about maps: the information they hold within their lines and symbols, the clues they contain about the times in which other people lived. A map is more than just . . . a map. It reveals the philosophy and history and technological advancement of its era. It reveals the fears and prejudices of its makers. It is a chronicle of place and past and purpose.

Maps can also be pretty to look at.

In 1981, I drove with my boyfriend from North Carolina to Los Angeles. In 1982, we drove from Los Angeles to New York City. He did the driving—all of it—and I read the flip book AAA made for us, mapping our entire journey in one-hundred-mile bullets. I was Vasco da Gama, he was Mario Andretti. We had a CB and our handle was "Double Trouble." We talked to long-distance truckers the whole way across and back. We learned that "bear in a brown wrapper" meant "policeman in an unmarked car." We learned that "What's it look like over your donkey?" meant "what have you passed? What's behind you?" And once, in Texas, we learned that "cow in the meridian" meant that there was a cow calmly grazing in the strip of grass separating East 80 from West 80.

It was those two cross-country adventures that sparked my fascination with reading maps. Every town we passed, every state park we drove through, every state line we crossed—everything was listed somewhere on some map. If I read the map correctly, I could find where we were and get us to where we needed to go. It was a wonderful discovery; words and icons and diagrams on a piece of paper became real, bustling, alive places.

I lose myself in fantasy while reading an atlas. Imagine! Every page, every map of India or Australia or Lake Erie or Hudson Bay or Mongolia—these places exist, right now. Right now coffee beans are growing in Brazil. Right now someone in Russia is having a birthday party. Right now someone in Chile is dying. Someone in Jamaica is falling in love. Someone in—well, you can continue this fancy yourself.

Here's a thought: As a writer, you are limited only by the expanse of your imagination and the length of your life. Your stories can take you anywhere you want to go. Anywhere.

For the Purposes of This Exercise

Pick a place and research it. They should be real, existing places, like Paris or Poughkeepsie. Find a map—start with a present-day map—and begin to investigate.

How big is this place?
How many people live there?
What is it like to live there?
What's the weather like?
What do people do there?
Is it prosperous/poor/pretty/pretty awful?
What's the good part of town? The bad?
Are there parks? Schools? Museums? Post offices?

If your place is larger than one town or city, try to find some specifics to show you've really got a feel for it. For example, if you're researching Australia, don't just say, "a whole continent" or "there are kangaroos."

You're at the helm here. If you want, you can swing the compass 180 degrees and shake things up. You can research London in the 1600s. You can describe Boston as it will be in the year 2100. You can describe a city in deepest China or in the place in which you grew up. Remember, with the possible exception of the most inner of monologues, physical place will impact everything you write.

This is not a subjective exercise, meaning that you are not trying for a description in any one person's *voice*. Of course, your exploration will be affected by your own style and slant, but the main point here is to build up a library of facts. If you give these exercises your best effort, you will have the beginnings of a great resource library made by you, for use in your writing. You may not want to write about Detroit today, but if you do spend some time researching it, you will have the information there ready for when you *do* need it. Trust me.

There is also something to be said for the discipline of research itself. Let's say you do this exercise ten or so times. You begin to realize that you like gathering information, flipping though maps, atlases, encyclopedias. You begin to get even more excited about the vast variety of this marvelous world. You look at your own city differently. You understand—you *really* understand—that the world is your oyster. You feel confident that, if you set your mind to it, you can investigate just about any subject well enough to write about it. Even astrophysics. Even Ancient Greek.

Even cartography.

A Small Snack

This is my belief: A small snack is one of life's great and enduring pleasures. In order to present this in a logical, mathematical format, I ask you to consider the following:

1. Life is hard.
2. Snacks are tasty.
3. Small snacks, artfully placed during the course of a hard day, therefore have the potential to cheer, hearten, promote good will, and help you keep your sense of humor, an essential tool in today's stressful, dehumanizing, loveless world.

Having said all that, I am more than willing to admit that food might mean more to me than it does to you. Perhaps you are one of these "I eat to stay alive and that's it" people. God bless you, and let's hope we never meet.

If you are NOT an "eat-to-live" person, then you might agree with the brilliant writer Oscar Wilde's precept: "I do so hate people who are casual about meals, *it's so shallow.*" You know the type he's talking about. "Oh, it was so busy today, I FORGOT TO EAT." "Look, it's just *dinner;* stop making such a fuss about where we go to eat." They say, life is short, food doesn't matter that much. I say, life is short, *everything*—including food—*matters that much.*

For the Purposes of This Exercise

Let's write about eating and food and meals. About how it all feels and tastes and smells and the rituals we ascribe and the comfort and security it brings to the end of a really rotten day.

As a writer, your powers of description are very important. In order to be able to describe, you must be able to observe, and in order to observe, you must be aware. Therefore, throughout this workbook, you are asked to notice your surroundings and write about them. How does it look where you are? How does it sound, smell, feel? Who is there with you? What are the people saying?

A baby learns to sit up, then crawl, then walk a few tentative, toddling steps. Everything in organic order, everything moving forward. In your development as a writer, there are organic, orderly steps that will help you toward realizing your ability and fulfilling your potential. If you can try to follow these steps, as aggravating and often frustrating as they are, your talent will develop and improve and evolve and grow. I promise. It sure won't be easy and it sometimes will seem like miserable work, but nothing of value comes easily—despite what they might suggest on television.

Your "baby steps" as a developing writer follow this basic formula:

1. How does "X" affect ME?
2. How does "X" affect other people around me (real/ fictional)?
3. How can I use "X" in a story, toward the formation of a character or a plot?

For example: A meal of significance.

Think back to your childhood. Do you remember a particular meal or snack or treat? A birthday cake? A horrible spinach/ cauliflower/liver fiasco you were forced to stare at for days and days as it formed into a yucky lump because you refused to eat it? A Mr. Softee ice cream, or a Dairy Queen, or a Good Humor snow cone? Write down as many food memories as you can recall. These will be useful to you in your writing. Maybe one day you will write about a kid, a kid who's eating a brownie—and there you are, in the moment, and it's real to you and it sounds real and it feels real to your readers.

Move up through to the present day. Keep a "food memories" journal. See if there are connections between meals and other moments in your life—a big family scene, a romance, a traumatic revelation. Do certain foods make you feel a certain way? Do you connect certain meals with a time of your life, a person in your life? Are there places in your heart that can only be *reached* by key lime pie? Go for that detail, research it the way a historian does a Civil War battle, experiment with it the way a physicist does with ions and magnets and black holes.

We need food to live. It is *vital,* in the most profound sense of the word. We are ALIVE, and every day we pay tribute to that fact by breathing and eating and sleeping and . . . other bodily functions.

As a writer you can USE this most fundamental, *essential* aspect of our lives: You can use it to mean MORE than it seems. Is food symbolic? You bet it is. Can the act of preparing food and eating it and sharing it with someone else be allegorical—can it be a *metaphor* for bigger and more complex issues?

Yes. Next question.

Remember:

I have done it.
I have observed it.
I can create it.

If only world peace was this simple. . . .

If Breakfast Be the Meal of Love

For the first thirty-two years of my life, I was a morning person. More often than not, I woke up in a basically good mood, anticipating the day, a day filled with possibilities, one more chance to get it right. I felt mentally and morally energetic, alert, and attentive. Ready for the challenge. Eager to participate. The promise of a new day . . .

Breakfast was a big component. I loved it. It was my favorite meal. Bagel, toast, muffin, fried eggs, french toast, pancakes, tasty, tasty, tasty. Hash browns. Maybe bacon. Also lots of coffee. A great deal of coffee.

Time passes. Things change. Now I'm a mom, insomnia has kicked in, and now I'm frequently tired and snappish in the morning. I'm not hungry first thing in the morning, so no breakfast until later. I often skip lunch and go right into an early dinner with the kids. Two meals compromised, and one at the end of the day when I'm—you guessed it—feeling tired and snappish again.

Meals are a big deal. Eating is a big deal. First off, there's the food itself. Everyone has likes and dislikes. People become aroused and stimulated by the aroma of a tasty snack they like, and they can feel disgusted or even nauseated by the smell of food they hate.

There's also the visual aspect. A plate of brownies looks exciting. A beautifully set table, well-presented meals, flowers—these things please our senses, appeal to our aesthetics. And let's not overlook the social aspect of eating. Family picnics, fancy restaurant dates, a bowl of spaghetti with a friend. Conversation and the dinner table; we sit together, sharing a communal event, talking and eating and eating and talking.

Sight, smell, social: These just graze the surface of the complex relationship we have with food.

It is, of course, possible that no one will ever eat in your stories. I've noticed that in more that one of the 1940s noir detective films *(The Big Sleep, Double Indemnity, Dial M for Murder)* no one ever seems to eat. Sure, they smoke and drink a lot—but no sitting down to a hearty beef stew. But then there are also films like *Babette's Feast* and *Tom Jones* and *Like Water for Chocolate* in which meals and their preparation play a major role. After seeing *The Scent of Green Papaya* I had a huge craving for Vietnamese cooking. And didn't the spread in *Big Night* look amazing?

Here's my point: Everybody eats. Writing about eating is a way to connect with your readers, draw them in. Food can be sensual, provocative, seductive. You can have a lot of fun describing a meal. Hemingway did. Describing a meal can also make your world seem real—"look, people EAT there, they're like you and me." Again, let me stress that it is an option never to have a hot sit-down or a cold stand-up in your stories. It's your choice. I believe that the event of having a meal is a way to add down-home ease to your story. But it is only one of many ways.

For the Purposes of This Exercise

Hopefully, in the previous exercise, "A Small Snack," you have put some thought into your own food history. You have written about meals of significance in your life. Now it's time to shift that sharpened awareness out into your busy world. First, look around you. What do other people like to eat? How do they eat? Do they eat gracefully, with table manners, enjoying both the social and gastronomic aspects of the meal? Or is it feeding time at the zoo—only just short of a feed bag or trough?

1. For a day, carry a pad or notebook around with you and jot down every encounter you have with other people eating. This will start to give you some honest and real examples to pull from when you are writing your own *Tom Jones* scenes. If you can, eat in

a restaurant—great people-watching there. Also the food courts in malls. It may surprise you, once you start looking, how much food is being consumed right out in the open every moment. Taxi drivers sip coffee and slam-eat danishes. Lonely widows and widowers eat alone, carefully spooning up their soup, counting the check out in coins. Kids are fully invested in whatever they are eating at that exact moment.

2. It's time, yet again, to look back on your favorite books and movies. And television. Even if one might consider TV to be a corrupt time-suck, there is no question that it is a big part of our culture. I live now, and I am affected by television. I know that reading is better, more productive and stimulating for my brain. But nothing is as relaxing as a good evening of NBC sitcoms or ABC dramas. And don't forget HBO!

Also, and this is really true, I learned how to write a complete tight, self-contained story from watching TV. The half-hour and the one-hour formats for both drama and comedy are fertile ground for plot junkies. These shows have a clear agenda: Within a limited amount of time they need to establish a beginning, middle, and end. They need to plant either dramatic or comedic details that will be paid off later in the show. Dialogue needs to further plot and character.

Once you've spent some time observing people around you eating, try going to the page or screen. Scrutinize a little there, too. For a day or so, write down examples of fictional people eating. Write down the name of the book, movie, or TV show. Who was in it? Who wrote it? Who ate what? Did it add to the story? Was it gratuitous? Was it gratuitous but pleasant and enjoyable?

After you have observed others eating and investigated the fictional food world around you for details about meals, snacks, cooking, and just general eating, it's time to take the next step.

3. Pick a character you know from a book or TV/movie, preferably one who does not eat in the story. Write a meal scene for them. Who is there? What do they eat? What is the setting? Is it a

humanizing event, like giving all the orphans from *Oliver Twist* their own cheese pizza? Is it romantic and sweet, like Jane Eyre and Mr. Rochester ordering in Chinese? You can really stretch your imagination with this one—there are no rules. The purpose is to practice getting fictional characters to eat. Yes, they also need to dress themselves and walk and talk and get into trouble, but all that in good time. Right now, it's about grilled flounder, rice, and peas.

4. Now you are well ready to practice writing a food scene from scratch. Use the observations you've collected, and the work you've done with existing characters. Set the table, plan the menu, invite the guests.

If you are already writing a piece, this is a good time to plumb the depths of your knowledge of the characters. If you never intended there to be a meal or even a cup of coffee in your story, perhaps you can approach this as purely a drill, like a scene in a movie destined for the cutting-room floor.

You might want to write about many different types of eating opportunities: all three basic meals, and tea time, and late-night snacking, and diet binges. Eating on the go. Lengthy, sit-down meals. Picnics. Eating in a car. In an airplane. Each scenario carries a unique set of feelings. Explore as many as you can. Does your character prefer to eat in bed? Does your character eat only a specific type of food, rigidly defined? There is character and plot to be found in these details. We reveal ourselves in everything we do.

Let me repeat that once more: *We reveal ourselves in everything we do.* So while on the surface it reads like a sandwich and a Coke, there are layers of unspoken incentives, silent intentions, implied inclinations. You are describing a bowl of oatmeal with your sister, a sister who resents you, a sister you do not trust with your new boyfriend, and all that will be coming out over brown sugar and raisins.

We reveal ourselves in everything we do.

Dyslexia and Other Physical Obstacles, or The Pen Is Mightier Than the Problem

There is always a moment during the New York City Marathon when the first wheelchair competitor comes into view. For a split second you can feel the crowd seize up—What do we *do?* Then a huge cheer erupts. I don't think it's because the spectators are uncomfortable. I think that it's because seeing someone in a wheelchair powering down the street reminds us of how *hard* some people have to work in order to profit from opportunities we have handed to us on a platter every waking day.

Until quite recently, dyslexia was not readily diagnosed in schoolchildren, and a great many of them grew up feeling slow and, tragically, stupid. As they struggled to read and write, their classmates sailed past them, enjoying learning, teasing little Billy or Alice for writing letters so funny. Many of these perfectly intelligent children simply gave up trying. They fell through the cracks and right out of the system altogether.

So let's say you have dyslexia or another learning disability or physical obstacle to overcome. You have my utmost respect. You have had to work twice as hard to master the basic tools of this writing trade. It may be extraordinarily hard for you to trust in your talent, to give yourself permission to take yourself seriously as a writer, because of years of feeling incapable, incompetent. You may have trouble letting your imagination stretch, uninhibited, because you are self-conscious about your spelling, your syntax, your handwriting.

This is my suggestion: Chances are, you've suffered enough. The clock is ticking. Put all that self-doubt behind you *just for to-*

day, and write what's in your heart. Hemingway used to say that he wrote every day until he wrote the *one true sentence,* and then he stopped. Don't worry about "Writing" (with a capital "W"). Just "write" (small "w"). Your situation is unique. Your experiences give you a way of looking at life that is different. So much of life is a drive toward fitting in, being homogenous. I say skip that. You're different. Write different.

ONE OTHER THOUGHT: George Balanchine, the ballet choreographer, had a great saying—"Comparison is Death." He was right. The minute we start measuring ourselves up against this person and that person, we lose that original admiration of our own work. Or—more to the point—we lose the blissful ignorance that blinds us to just how damn hard it is to make it as a writer. Don't ask, don't tell. Just pick up the pen, throw a towel over your emotional mirror, and write, write, write. There is a reason for your being exactly where you are *today.* All we need to do is show up, do the work, and drink coffee.

The rest will make sense in due time.

Your Daily Grind

Family can be the bane of a writer's existence: pushing us when we need to be left alone, criticizing us when only a few words of encouragement could get a person up on their feet and moving. Those people closest to us are often the worst critics of our abilities—perhaps because they expect more from us, and perhaps because they feel that, if they don't set us straight about our obvious shortcomings, no one will. Either way, a family member's disapproval can be devastating.

There is no doubt in my mind that my early attempts at short stories, screenplays, and novels were horrendous. The characters were stilted and flat, the use of adjectives excessive. One story in particular stirred up my sister's ire: In it, one character bluntly asks another, "So, what's your daily grind?" In the fifteen years since, she has hardly let an opportunity go by to remind me of this catastrophic insult to the writing profession. "Your daily grind" has come to symbolize everything I find pitiful about my early attempts to tell a story.

Still, here we are, years later, with a desire to become better writers. Back to the daily grind.

It occurs to me that a broad knowledge of (or at least a working vocabulary and the balls to fake a broad knowledge of) as many different types of jobs, trades, and occupations as possible is a great asset to any writer. Perhaps a character in your story is a truck driver. Or a surgeon. Or a waitress. Or a brick layer. Or a painter. Or a cook. Or a pirate. Your research into these fields will add credibility and depth to your work. If you can write confidently and with veracity about the daily world of a dentist, your story involving the love affair between a dentist and, say, a pirate, will sound real to the reader. They will be able to lose themselves in your story; they will trust you and believe in the world you have created.

For the Purposes of This Exercise

This exercise requires that you do a little homework. Read, ask questions, observe, use your imagination.

1. Pick a profession, and write about it for half an hour or more. What is the job like? How does one get this job? What's the pay like? The environment? The hours? The risk? Why would anyone want it? What is it like to be a . . . (fill in the blank). The more "daily grinds" you are knowledgeable about, the more fun you can have peopling your worlds. After all, not everyone wants to be a lawyer, doctor, or policewoman, never mind what the network television executives might have us believe.

2. Now it's time to personalize the research you have just done. Pick two or three of the jobs you investigated in section 1, and write about your imagined experience in that field. Describe what it was that drew you to this occupation. Was it hard to get a job in this area? Describe a day in your new position. What are your responsibilities? Do you like working in this profession? Imagine that this has been your career for many years. How do you feel about it long term? Are you good at it? Does it wear well?

3. One last activity. Think of at least ten famous people you know who are well-established in their respective fields: for instance, Francis Ford Coppola, filmmaker; Charles Dickens, writer; Paul McCartney, singer/songwriter; Frank Lloyd Wright, architect. Assess what you think to be their basic skills and conceive of a completely different field in which their abilities could be used. If you are feeling ambitious, do this same project for some fictional characters with whom you are well versed.

These occupational gymnastics might seem to be silly or pointless, but they will provide you with a broad, flexible perception of people's "employment" potential. You won't have to think of your characters in one, rigid, limited job capacity. This exercise begins your road to a deep, empathetic understanding of human abilities.

A Day in the Life

You sit down to face a blank page. The whiteness of it blazes up at you. You take up your pencil and stare at the empty, teasing, beckoning lines. Where to start?

You will write many stories in your hopefully long career as a writer. Some of your stories will be autobiographical by intention, some by accident. If you are a lawyer, some of your characters are likely to be lawyers—giving you the chance for deep insights into that profession. But will *all* your characters be lawyers?

As you set out to outline your plot, you will consider many, many elements of the world you want to create. Who lives there? Where is there? What do people do there during the day? Or the night? If your story has fourteen characters in it, do they all work in the same field? Or will you be doing a Richard Scarry *Busy, Busy World* extravaganza—doctor, lawyer, Indian chief, soldier, sailor?

Your characters will often have jobs, and those jobs will sometimes define them and how they behave. However, there is more to life than *work,* more to life than the job we do to pay our bills and put food on the table. People engage in hobbies, leisure pastimes, they contribute time and money to charities and organizations that mean something to them. By filling in the details that color a character's life, a writer allows the reader to view that character as a full, three-dimensional person. Even if these details never make it to the final draft of your story, at least you know them, and they serve as stock and spice for the stew you are creating.

This is not to say that every story written has to be part textbook, educating the reader, with a three-part quiz at the end. But the true joy of writing is the freedom it gives the writer, and then later the reader, to experience worlds beyond our own.

If you are interested in the American Wild West, yours is the freedom to dive headlong into books and photographs and movies and whatever you can find to open that world up to you— learn, absorb, assimilate, understand. Then take what you know, shake it down, cut it up, bend the corners to fit, and bingo. You have a passionate and fascinating story about Violet Chuttlebort and her struggle to hang onto her four hundred thousand-acre cattle farm in Wyoming. Is Violet a little bit you? Of course. Do you live in Wyoming? Probably not. Probably the closest you've ever come to cattle is watching John Ford's *The Searchers* . . . and that's just fine. Writers are the great pretenders. Imagination is the greatest password of them all.

For the Purposes of This Exercise

Establish a character and his or her basic profession, if indeed you want your character to have a traditional job at all. THEN, fill in the space around him or her. What does your character do with his or her free time? Where does he or she go on vacations? Does your character collect anything? Does your character have a particularly self-destructive habit, say like excessive drinking, gambling, drugs? Is he or she a healthy soul, committed to exercise, eating three pieces of fruit a day, and studying yoga?

Does your character like to read books? Go to movies? Does he or she grow plants? Is your character a good cook? There are endless combinations of behaviors and approaches to life. Is your character politically involved? Does he or she vote? Does he or she spend time registering voters or canvassing for a census or teaching at a literacy program? Does he or she have a dog? A bird? A lizard?

This is a good follow-up to "Your Daily Grind." Now that you have spent time researching a character's profession, try to imagine what the rest of his or her life will be like. Take yourself through twenty-four hours in your character's day. The more specific and the less romantic and idealized you can be about the responsibilities and pitfalls of that life, the more rich and compelling your writing will be.

As an example: Let's say you're a twenty-six-year-old single man writing about a thirty-six-year-old divorced mother of two, and you want it to sound real. Clearly, you can't write from personal experience. What to do?

You can do some basic reading—*What to Expect When You're Expecting* and some child-care books and some "How to Handle a Truly Nightmare Child"–type books might be helpful. If you have a female relative or friend with young children, ask them if you can spend time with them and ask lots of questions. Observe, take notes. Ask around and find out if your friends or relatives know other women with young children and ask if you can talk to them. Tell them you're writing a story. There are so many ways to research. And then there is imagination.

There are those who maintain with absolute assurance the dictum that you must only write about what you know. That anything else is false and will sound false and no one will enjoy reading it. I recently endured an unpleasant evening with a gentleman (kind assessment) who took it upon himself to rip several of my short stories into tiny little shreds, being under the faulty assumption that he was doing me a favor. He kept holding up the one autobiographical story of mine that he had read, lecturing on and on . . . "Why don't you just write about your own world? Why don't you just write about what you've experienced? Why would you ever consider writing about anything that you hadn't personally done/seen/lived/eaten/worn? . . ."

It was a lousy evening. He also couldn't cook.

Needless to say, the literary world would consist of about fifteen books if people only ever wrote about their exact personal experiences. This guy didn't get the basic equation of writing:

A writer takes their frame of reference

ADDS
their particular understanding of the world at that given time

APPLIES IT

to each and every situation and person and emotion about which they choose to write

AND THIS RESULTS IN . . .
a story.

writing = the known + the imagined

If it's just the known, it will be limited; and if it's just the imagined, it will be artificial.

The things that you come up with can be written on index cards and kept for future stories . . . you never know when your idea about a character's bottle-top collection might just make a certain story sing.

The Time of Their Lives

The nature versus nurture debate is an old one. Are we delivered into this world a blank slate, without personality, without a predisposition toward any habits, abilities, illnesses, traits? Or are we hardwired from the moment of conception, fated to be a distinct and exact individual with no chance of environmental influence? Is it genes or genitors?

The best argument I have ever heard on this topic suggested this: At any given moment of our lives, we represent 100 percent nature interacting with 100 percent nurture. We are the unique combination of our own particular mixed bag of nuts. How we react to any given scenario is the sum of who we are chemically, what we have experienced emotionally, and the hopefully increasingly broad base of reference material stored in our brains. Result: ME. Or in your case, YOU.

We are, without doubt, affected by many, many elements of our surroundings: our present and past locations, the weather, movies, music, books, the political atmosphere, clothes, television, etc. These influences shape our behavior, and, in turn, our behavior affects how other people react to us, treat us, include *or* exclude us. We bring to the table who we are: Depending on what's being served, we might enjoy the meal or come away with massive indigestion.

Right now, let's talk about one specific influence: *time.*

I'm sure that you have heard the expression, "So-and-So was simply born *before their time.*" This has always interested me—the concept that a particular person, due to their temperament, would have been better off had they been born in a different era. This implies that time is also a factor in shaping our personality. Could a person's disposition jar with the 1990s, but be completely at home during the 1890s? Could the type of writing or composing or choreographing a person is compelled to create simply not fit in, not belong during the 1700s, but be acceptable and desirable now? This is an intriguing question.

This exercise asks you to consider options and how they are affected by the times during which we live. It is possible that all of your stories will be set during the here and now, but perhaps you will choose to walk backward down memory lane or shoot fast forward into the unwritten future. It will be helpful to spend some time stretching your time line as wide as it can go. What was life like during the Egyptian era? Or in China during the 1950s? What will it be like in San Francisco in the year 2300?

This is a research-oriented exercise. Pick a time, a century if your examination is broad, or a specific year or even day if it is narrow. You will have to pick a *place* as well, as the 1920s were without a doubt different in Baltimore and Bora Bora. Do some study and begin to collect details about daily life in that place during that time. What did people wear? How did they get around? What did they eat, read? How was their medical care? What was important to people then? There are thousands of questions to ask. Try to imagine what a day in their life was, or will be, like.

This exercise benefits from curiosity. See if you can find any pictures (if they exist) of your place of choice during that time. Who were the political leaders (if any)? How were people educated (if they were)? Make a list of ten to twenty questions about that time, and then set out to answer them. You might want to keep your list of questions so you can use them again next time you do this exercise.

A WORD TO THE WISE: You and I both know that books exist already in great numbers, some fiction, some nonfiction, describing life during different times. Why not just use these existing books if and when you need them?

I'll tell you why: Writing is practice, practice, practice. Do you think Mark Spitz said, "Oh, well, I'm not going to swim against the clock if I don't have to. I know how to swim, and I know how to tell time. That's good enough for me." He most certainly did not! He practiced swimming against the clock at every possible opportunity. He wanted to be ready. He wanted to challenge himself. Someone told me once that, in tennis, the difference between an "A" player and a "B" player is this: *An "A" player ALWAYS goes for the ball.*

So, yes, you can simply buy the research books and use them if and only if you need them. Or you can set goals, push yourself, set new goals, and push yourself again. Write as much as you can every day. Write about different people, places, times. Write about men and women and children and adults and sick people and healthy people and people you love and people you despise.

In other words . . . *go for each and every ball.*

The Wrong Date and Time

A good friend of mine, let's call her Sophie, told me this story. Sophie is an attractive, intelligent woman in her early forties. She is single. She didn't date often; certainly not because of any failing on her part, but rather due to the quality of available men. One night, Sophie went on a first date with a seemingly nice lawyer. They had dinner, they talked, and it came time to wrap things up. He offered to escort her to her home in Brentwood. Nice guy? You be the judge.

As the two of them walked up the path to her front door, Sophie in the front and the lawyer bringing up the rear, she heard the *unmistakable sound of* . . . a spray of breath freshener. Then another. Sophie's blood ran cold: What was this guy's plan? Did he have an expectation of intimacy? She was mortified. Did he expect a kiss? An embrace? Or . . . *more?* She bid a rapid good night and thank you and fled inside.

Not all dates are bad, but all bad dates are pretty much the same. It's a mathematical equation: Add a cup of incompatibility to a dash of rudeness, a sprig of bad breath (or the alternate breath freshener), and a pinch of unbelievable boredom. The recipe adds up to an evening better spent walking on broken glass.

For the Purposes of This Exercise

1. Think back to some of your own less-than-wonderful dates, encounters, back-fired assignations. Describe in as much detail as you can what each date was like. Spare no particulars. Remember, you never know when some hideous infraction, caused even possibly by yourself, will define a character for your next story.

People are fascinating all by themselves: When two or more of them are together, the level of mesmerizingly sordid humanity skyrockets. How do we behave ourselves when the attraction is nonexistent? What is it about another person that repulses, or bores, or irritates us? These are all things to consider, record, and remember.

So try to recall as many bad datelike encounters as you can. Dredging up these undesirable memories may seem masochistic, but that comes with the territory: As a writer, you've got to get in the habit of harvesting *all* the acreage. The pretty flowers are great, but the bent and twisted and screwy ones are more interesting.

2. This is where your imagination comes into play. After you've spent some time summoning up your own personal dates-from-hell, get ready to invent some. Go wild. Describe a date between two known characters, real or fictional—say, Archie Bunker and Queen Latifah. Albert Einstein and Charo. Carrot Top and Meryl Streep. What do they talk about? Where do they go? What do they do? Who pays? Remember, these are *bad* dates we're putting together.

You certainly do not have to use real people if you don't want to. Perhaps you'll fool around with some characters from a story you're working on. Or two (or three . . .) people you pluck from thin air. The point isn't really *who* is on this date, but how they react to each other and how the evening (or day?) unfolds. There are no rules.

This exercise, like so many others, may seem puzzling at first. What is the benefit of describing a bad date? Why not just focus on happy people? Isn't it important to concentrate on cheerful, optimistic, joyful encounters?

Yes, it is. We are taught from birth to highlight the good; our culture doesn't like to talk about death, emotional difficulties, intellectual dilemmas. It would not be considered at all odd to study a successful relationship. It is considered "negative" to dwell on the mistakes we make and have to live with, or the cruelties we inflict, or the really just plain nasty side of human behavior. It exists, yes, but let's just not *dwell* on it.

My mother was a fascinating woman for many reasons, not the

least of which was that she was able to read two newspapers and watch the news on TV twice a day *and have absolutely NO idea what was going on in the world.* I asked her once why she skimmed over the unpleasant bits and she frowned at me. "Oh, Caroline," she sighed. "*Why?* I don't like all the disagreeable things. They're so *unamusing.*"

This is perhaps exactly why I find myself drawn to the dark side of the human heart. I had to find my own flashlight.

Got yours?

Objects of Desire

Are you home? Look around. What do you see? Go into your kitchen. Make a mental list of *things* you have there, appliances, small electrical machines we use every day and don't pay much mind. Your toaster. Your refrigerator. Oven. Microwave. Blender. Juicer. Mixer. Ice machine. Small television to watch Jerry Springer while you peel the potatoes. Or, perhaps, electric potato peeler (Do they make those?).

Now imagine yourself on a desert island in a small grass hut. You wake up, greet the tropical morning with a vigorous smile and then make—*what?* Coffee? Don't think so. Orange juice? Buttered toast? Nope. Then you . . . take a shower? No running hot water. No clean clothes. No iron. No fabric softener. Can't listen to the radio. Can't read the paper. No TV for darn sure.

Our daily lives are touched—no—enveloped by gadgets. Our basic needs are constrained by the inventions of the past one hundred years: Even the most basic battery has us by the throat. Are we helpless? Weakened by the necessities of our daily habits? Can I live without Canada Dry seltzer, Starbuck's house blend (ground for a melita drip), and five-minute boiled eggs? Technically, yes. But my desert island existence would be grim.

Some of your stories will be more detail oriented than others. One might focus on a trim black lizard watch strap. Another might address world peace. I certainly cannot predict the degree to which your writing style will pitch inward or outward; whether your search for self-expression will address the universal through the specific or the other way around. Are you a person who focuses on particulars? How much detail do you notice on average? The forest or the trees?

My husband and I have very different styles of observation. We can both be in the same room and come away with completely different impressions: He will remember the exact color of the wallpaper, how many lamps there were and what they looked like, the fashion and positioning of the furniture, the colors of people's clothing. All I can do is tell you what everyone said. People observe and attend to their surroundings in ways that reflect and reveal how their minds work.

As a writer, you will spend a lifetime sharpening your observational skills. The more you are aware of, the more you can write about: AWARE with your eyes, with your heart, your soul, your body. The world is out there for you to gather up and hold. You are on a lifetime mission. Your assignment: *Live and observe.* Your objective: *experience.* The end result? Hopefully, lots and lots and lots of wonderful stories.

The first order of business is to notice your surroundings. Your home. Start there. What is in your room—apartment—house—tent—mobile home—ancestral mansion? Your abode? Your residence? Look around. Get a pencil and a piece of paper and go to work.

For the Purposes of This Exercise

1. Make a complete list of the everyday, utilitarian stuff in your home, for example, your bed. Next to each item, rate its degree of necessity, meaning, to what extent could you live without it. This will start you on a path of attentiveness. How many times a day do you really *notice* your air conditioner? How many times a day do you walk by it, see it, hear it running? How *aware* are you of your surroundings?

To be oblivious is insidious: If we allow things to be invisible to us, what's to stop people and places from going unnoticed as well? If we force ourselves to be alert, to live consciously in our daily movements, we are establishing a routine of heightened awareness.

This exercise does not mean to imply that an awareness of one's surroundings must manifest itself in all your work. It need not. Your commitment to developing a watchful eye will pay off nonetheless.

2. Once you've made a list of items in your home and rated their "essential-ness," widen the search. Observe other people's homes/work places. Look at homes on television and in movies. Write down what you see and remember. Think about homes you encounter in books or short stories. What particulars are other writers including? Also, consider the characters in your own works. Even if you weren't planning on describing their homes in detail, try to flesh out their physical worlds. Do they have a four-slice toaster?

How about trends? Have you begun to notice similarities in the way in which people lay out their kitchens? Do most apartments have a television in the living room but not a bookshelf? Do more married people have pets? Is there more art on the walls in the homes of your single friends or married friends?

Look, see, observe, record. Write.

Reuse, Rethink, Recycle

April 1970. The *Apollo* 13 mission was in grave trouble, the folks at Mission Control had to think fast and think smart. The moon landing was now aborted, the astronauts were in danger, and it *looked* as if they might not make it back to Earth. In order to bring our brave boys home alive, the crew back at NASA had to be nimble, be quick, and readjust their thinking.

Reconsider: The command module and the LEM were made with one purpose in mind—to take three guys from the Earth to the moon and back—they now had to envision a *new* purpose, a *different* function for the same mechanism. Could it be done? It was done.

Sometimes we need to completely "reapproach" a situation. We need to step back and look at what's going on with a fresh eye. How do we learn to reuse, rethink, recycle? Do we need to be in a crisis condition in order to really drop our set opinions and strategies and start afresh?

Sometimes we don't need to reinvent the wheel, we just need to turn it over and look at it from a new perspective. Give the brain a jolt. A wake-up cup of coffee for the creative consciousness. As a writer, it is imperative that you keep a keen and open mind. It's a horrible thought, but what would have happened if the NASA folks had said to Jim Lovell, Jack Swaggert, and Fred Haise, "Well, we're sorry, but the LEM is designed for landing on the moon, NOT for bringing the three of you back to Earth, so awfully sorry and good-bye"?

For the Purposes of This Exercise

Let's think about our traditional tales, our seemingly "universal" fables, and then let's think about them again. Differently.

Let's not so much REINVENT the wheel as REPOSITION the wheel.

1. Make a list of the fables and folk tales and fairy tales and legends and cautionary stories of our childhood, hopefully a good long list. Include any epics, ballads, sagas, and myths you remember from the campfire/night-light. Then as best as you can, describe the basic plot in two or three sentences. THEN, after that, define the MORAL of this tale.

I suggest you make a chart with three columns: TITLE, PLOT, MORAL. Try to include as many examples as you remember.

If your recall is limited, or if you watched more television than you care to admit as a child, this is now the time to do some research. There are many, many books on fairy tales—Grimms, Aesop's, Mother Goose—to name just three. Also, there are great collections out there that present these stories by *country*, by historical period, by religious belief. Try to come up with at least fifteen or twenty tales.

2. Look at the plot descriptions of these folk tales. Do any of them look familiar? Look carefully over your list and begin to compare them with movies/books you know. Next to each one of the fifteen or twenty stories you have analyzed, write down any OTHER plots you recognize as being drawn from/derivative of/similar to these. The fairy tale is the foundation; the modern-day novel, movie, or TV show is the offspring.

The study of folklore *is* the study of literature.

In the end you will have made a carefully considered list of traditional stories from your childhood and your culture, and you will have made an analysis of those stories. You have listed the plots and the morals and lessons to be learned. You will have reflected upon the universal applications of these "*uber* stories." Have you seen Hansel and Gretel in any *other* story you have read/seen? A young brother and sister, abandoned by a weak father and cruel stepmother, are led into the woods to die, only to be found by an evil witch with bad intentions of her own? They triumph by killing the witch, thereby freeing themselves. They return home to a father who now wants them and loves them and all is well and happy.

OK, well, it's not *Braveheart,* but keep looking. The Apollo guys didn't give up trying. They kept looking and looking until they saw another way. Don't throw out that wheel. Chop it up into tiny bread-crumb-size pieces and use it to find your way home. . . .

Writer's Block, or Surviving a Big Chill

This is a slippery one. The name implies that the material is there, ready and able, but there exists a horrible, stubborn, separate-from-you obstruction. It's like the Dutch boy and his finger having separate DNA.

However, we all know that's not the case. Writers claiming "writer's block" are speaking to a myriad of issues. Are they really completely out of ideas? Have they grown tired of the particular subject about which they write, making it damn near impossible to get excited about imagination or inspiration knocking at their door? Are there *other issues* in their lives that are clouding the mind, providing frequent distractions? Can one get "unblocked"?

I believe that there are times in every profession in which it's possible to feel burned out. Used up. I believe that writer's block can happen for this reason. I also believe that there are times when we get close to something, times when the intensity meter is turned way up and things can get pretty uncomfortable. I believe that writer's block can happen for this reason, too. Sometimes it is important to take a break, get recharged, and then hop back in the saddle. And, loathe as I am to say this, sometimes there might be a more serious message behind the feeling of being "blocked."

It is up to you to judge whether you need a mental/physical change of scene, a break, or a new profession. In the meantime, why not drink a lot of coffee and try to keep on with your journal pages, so you won't get completely out of "shape." Trust your instincts. You'll know when it's time to pace yourself and when it's time to push yourself. Just don't give up and rush to surrender.

NO ONE SAID THIS WOULD BE EASY!!

Writing is hard work. Sometimes you'll feel like you're not doing it right because it is such heavy going. Welcome to the club. This is a constant challenge.

ONE OTHER THOUGHT: If you are pushing yourself way too hard, your brain may instinctively "shut down" in an attempt to get you to chill. You'll try to write, but nothing comes out: The faucet has been turned off, off, off. This will also seem like "writer's block." This happened to a good friend of mine. It was only *after* he stopped trying to write "the Great American Novel" and started to write what he felt passionately about that the work began to pour out of him. At first he felt like he had failed. He felt that by not constantly pushing himself to achieve, achieve, achieve, he had let down the team. In fact, he had released the chokehold, pulled out his "finger." The dam did break, and he was almost drowned by more material than he could write in a lifetime.

No, he was not Dutch.

Pay No Attention to the Man Behind the Curtain

The Compact Oxford English Dictionary describes an onion as "having a swollen bulb with many concentric layers." A good friend of mine from college once confessed—granted, it *was* after a late night of revelry and *no sleep*—that, as a child, she had thought the dictionary read "having a swollen bulb with many *eccentric* layers."

Change one word, change the meaning. However, whether they are *concentric* or *eccentric,* it is agreed that the onion has layers. We peel off the outer layers most often when cooking. Then, depending on the appearance of the now exposed onion and the requirements of the recipe, we may stop uncovering then and there, or we may continue pulling off layer after layer, chopping and dicing, unmasking the true onion within for all to see. It's an ugly business, I agree, but someone has to do it.

Are we onionlike? Do we have layers? I believe that we do. We can be guarded, cautious—playing close to the vest and watching others to gauge their move first. As we feel more comfortable with the situation and/or people at hand, we may choose to let down our defenses a touch. Some people see only the very small part of us that we judge to be fit for public consumption; other people can see right through whatever shields we repeatedly try to put up. Some defenses work at keeping people out. Others are effective at turning us into prisoners.

Degrees, volumes, temperature, and effectiveness aside, we have all got many different layers to our personalities. Some develop with age and experience. Some come right into the world with us on day one. They add depth to our character. They make us more complex, more interesting. Some people are increasingly fascinating the more time you spend with them. Wonder why? It's because more and more of their personalities are revealed (uncovered) as you get to know them. They are not an open book. They *are* a dark horse. They have secrets. We want to know them.

For the Purposes of This Exercise

Let's consider people and the many layers of their personalities. Let's allow that people might *hide* parts of their character, and let's even suggest that sometimes, *maybe,* people lie.

Let's focus for a moment on the stuff that we hide. And the reasons that we hide.

1. Make a list of five real people you know well, and five characters from TV or books or movies with whom you are well-versed. Each person gets an index card, with their name on the top left corner. Then, try to fill up the index card describing as many layers of their personality as you can peel away. Make sure to note if this is a layer that the person in question intends for you to see or not.

For example: Pee Wee Herman (fictional).

1. Seems to be stuck in preadolescent phase/childlike emotions, perhaps hiding traumatic experience.
2. Lives alone with gadgets and strange animals (note, make sure to investigate relationship with mother).
3. Is presexual energy responsible for pathological attachment to bicycle?
4. Ill-fitting clothes, all too small and tight. Examine Pee Wee Herman's need for infantilization/domination.
5. Seems friendly, all of the townsfolk like him; possible run-for-political-office in the future?
6. Likes music, loves to dance.
7. Seems to spend his days in playful gamboling: what of a ca-

reer, taking on adult responsibilities? Will Pee Wee remain immature man-boy forever?

Do this exercise a few times until you feel comfortable probing deep and deeper into a character's life story. Have fun, but keep in mind that we all bury stuff for a reason: We don't want anyone to dig it up.

We hide aspects of our past about which we are less than proud. We hide sides of our personalities about which we are embarrassed, frightened, uncomfortable. You are donning a surgical mask and gloves and taking a scalpel to the psyche.

Sure, everyone plays junior psychiatrist now and then. As a writer, you are a sort of shrink-priest-creator; the more time you spend in the study of human behavior, the more depth and detail you will be able to provide for your OWN writing.

Why do we hide parts of ourselves from those around us? How much time do you have for the answer to this one? We hide because to reveal would cost us. We hide because we want to control the way we are perceived. Because we want to appear strong, wise, sexy, more successful, more mature, young, innocent. We hide and we lie and we rewrite and we conceal and then we turn to our closest love, our dearest most beloved, and smile. Why do we smile? Because we believe that happy people are more honest? Because we think we're getting away with it? Because, as my mother said so often, You either laugh or you cry?

You've had some practice scrutinizing specific characters for their hidden layers. Now it's time to work from the inside out.

What do people hide? What do people want? What would a person spend a lifetime concealing? What would a person take to their grave without revealing? These elements, these secrets, they make a character interesting. They are the WHY and the WHAT FOR, coming after the WHO and the WHEN. Rhett loved Scarlett, sure, that was obvious. But what about the less obvious reason why Scarlett didn't love him back? Sergeant Brody goes out on his quest with Matt Hooper and Quint: The factual hunt itself is less compelling than the awareness that Brody hates the water, can't swim, and must overcome these fears in order to succeed in killing the shark.

2. Take a piece of paper. At the top, write down the name of a fictional character you know well. Write down something they might keep hidden—*and why.* Then elaborate. Work this into a full character description. Is there a chance for resolution to their issue—and if so, what would the circumstances of this redemption be? After you have done this a few times, try to create both character and secret. What kind of person would keep this kind of secret? What kinds of secrets do people tend to keep, to conceal from their loved ones, to take to the grave? This exercise can be worked from either end: what is concealed, and who conceals it.

This is a complicated exercise, but I hope that you will find it to be very rewarding. Writers are reflective and resourceful people. We search for answers, and where there are none, we make them up.

Triple Dare/Triple Scare, or How Low Will You Go?

Have you ever read a book in which a character was so naughty, so mean-spirited, malevolent, and vengeful . . . that you couldn't put it down?

The same is true with movies and television. Remember Catherine's father, the heartless Dr. Sloper in *Washington Square*? Napoleon the pig in *Animal Farm*? The Vicomte de Valmont in *Dangerous Liaisons*? Simon LeGree in *Uncle Tom's Cabin*? Captain Ahab in *Moby Dick*? Humbert Humbert in *Lolita*? Simon and Ralph in *Lord of the Flies*? The list is longer than you might think but not too long as to surprise you. People can do nasty things to one another. We are capable of immeasurable horror and cruelty. We can be motivated simply by pain and pleasure: moving away from pain and toward pleasure.

I am sure that you would not deny that wickedness is interesting. As characters in a book, happy, optimistic, and opportune people are flat out dullsville. THAT IS . . . unless the character starts out all cheerful and chipper, and as the story progresses, they get all manner of crap dumped on them until their sunny disposition turns cynical and bitter. *That* would keep my attention: a slow descent into hell.

If you have decided to create a character who will be a cursed blight on others in your story, it is necessary that you know what has brought him or her to this spot. Even if your readers will never know the back story, YOU need to know it. *Why* does little Barry pull whiskers off kittens? *Why* does twenty-five-year-old Arlene steal money from her poor grandmother? *Why* does a group of young boys gang up on one defenseless young girl?

It's so much easier to pretend that we don't have a dark side, but we do. Sometimes it just takes one person to set up a disgusting little vicious hell all around them and soak in it. Get too close and—look—now you're soaking in it, too. You may never create a truly evil character for your stories. You may never create a nasty, dishonest, mean character either. But if you decide to write more than half of one short story, chances are you will eventually have a less savory person living in your storyland.

This exercise will give you room to experience writing about "bad guys." Remember, this is a safe place. Just because you write about an unpleasant type of person, or just because you choose to populate your stories with undesirable, savage, and malicious characters, does not mean that you are like them. It does not say that you are destined to become like them. It only means that you are a writer, and that you are not afraid to confront the hidden and heartless side of inhuman behavior.

For the Purposes of This Exercise

1. Write about some less-than-wonderful things you have done in your life. Go into as much detail as you feel comfortable with. List your misdeeds chronologically. After you have recorded each event, describe how you felt afterward. Were there any consequences? If not, should there have been?

2. Write about some less-than-wonderful things you have thought about, fantasized about, or even written about in your journal—but that you never did. Why did you hold back? Are you glad, now, that you did?

3. In your immediate circle of friends and family, see if you can come up with a true list of bad behavior. Extend the list out a bit if need be. Include people you know only peripherally, and friends-of-friends. Write down their misdeeds, and, next to each one, write a sentence or two about your feelings and reactions.

4. Using examples from today's news, history books, and your own oral history (country and family), come up with some

examples of sinful, sinister, and immoral acts. Anyone who's studied the French Revolution in high school knows that people were every bit as nasty and dishonest and conniving back then. They just did it without benefit of television or automatic weapons.

5. Now that you've gotten a good feel for recording real-life depravity, let's turn to fiction. If you have ever had to make a list of heros and heroines throughout literature, now's your chance to do the opposite. Go through your books and make a list of all the nasty, hateful, and corrupt characters. (Try to include some of the classics you have read.) Describe their evil deeds. What did they do and why did they do it? Does their motivation make sense to you? Does it give a charge to the story? Or could the treachery and violence be gratuitous—put in the story just to titillate the watch-the-car-accident side of our personality?

6. You've looked into your own heart, then around you, and then into books, etc., for signs of depravity. Now you should match these ideas up with inspiration and write your own nasty/evil/cruel/mean person. Create a character and put him or her into a morality-testing situation. What happens? Does the character tuck the comic books under his or her sweater and make a break for the door? Does he or she return the wallet to the police department? Or does he or she leave the room and not shoot the spouse and children in a rage? These are choices, and our choices define us.

These don't have to be long scenes. Nothing epic. Just create a character and concoct an evil world around them. As you know, people are capable of amazing stuff. *Amazing*—dishonest beyond belief, greedy beyond belief, barbarous and brutal.

You could also try playing junior psychiatrist for a spell. Take a few of the characters you came up with and spend a page or so reflecting on how they got that way. Nature? Nurture? Pretend you are conducting a psyche work up for the police department.

Clinically analyze Hannibal Lecter from *The Silence of the Lambs*. Or the Big Bad Wolf from "Little Red Riding Hood." Come up with a theory or two as to why they turned out *so bad*.

Let's not forget, as Dorothy Parker once said, "If you have nothing nice to say . . . sit by me!"

The Wrong Brother

After the fiasco of my first screenplay, *The Winner,* I decided that it might be a good thing to learn the actual conventions and customs used when writing a script.

I signed on with Jeff Gordon—his "Writer's Boot Camp" was just starting up in Los Angeles. Under his wise and encouraging tutelage, I wrote three more screenplays, one about a female Cyrano de Bergerac called *Improving Mr. Fish* and one about a female Pygmalion called *Adder Island.* The last of the three, *Kill Devil Hill,* I wrote in 1992 about Orville and Wilbur, the Wright Brothers of Dayton, Ohio.

The latter was my best one. I researched it for nine months, reading just about everything I could get my hands on about the brothers and the circumstances that led them, after everyone had tried and failed, on December 17, 1903, to get the first heavier-than-air craft up and keep it up for twelve seconds. Amazing. I felt that the true story of Orville and Wilbur had never been told. We had all been sold a bill of goods, and I was going to pull back the curtains to reveal that . . . It was really *Wilbur* who did it all. However, after he died prematurely in 1912, Orville went on to live thirty-six years more, without his older brother. Between the years 1912 and 1948, *Orville refused to release the research papers, documents, and notes that Wilbur had so painstakingly kept throughout the years 1898 to 1912 . . . the years when everything was discovered, tested, and perfected by* Wilbur. The Library of Congress wanted Wilbur's papers and Orville said NO. The Smithsonian wanted Wilbur's papers and Orville said NO. Why?

I believe that it was self-preservation. If people saw the documents, recorded so meticulously by the scientifically minded Wilbur, they would instantly have known the truth: It was Wilbur, *not* Orville and Wilbur. Sure, Orville was always there. He was younger, stronger. He had more energy, more charisma. But when it came to the brains, the ideas, the logical and tenacious, scientific thinking—that was Wilbur.

By the time Orville died in 1948, the myth was well-created. In the public's mind, it was a two-man team, two determined and relentless brothers toiling side-by-side: Orville and Wilbur. We will always think of them as a pair, equally invested. How long does it take for a lie to take hold? Apparently thirty-six years is long enough.

I researched for nine months and wrote for two months, and it was finally completed. I asked my good friend and screen-writing mentor Brian Helgeland to give it a read and tell me his honest response. I respected—and still do respect—his opinion implicitly, so I was anxious to hear his thoughts.

Brian read *Kill Devil Hill* overnight and called me the next morning (please take note of the postscript about reading other people's work and responding promptly). "It's okay," he spoke carefully, letting me down easy. "It's okay, really, but—you're not going to want to hear this—I believe you wrote the story about *the wrong brother.*"

In his own clever way, Brian—a master storyteller himself—kindly explained that I had made a mistake in making Wilbur the central character. "Orville is the screwup," he said. "And the screwup is always the more interesting character. Always."

I had written *Kill Devil Hill* about the wrong brother. After ten minutes of panic and despondency, I thought about what Brian had said. He was, of course, 100 percent right. I had become too invested in the work, I had lost perspective. I took a short step back and could see the forest again. Orville. The story was really about the brother who *didn't* do the work. What was it like for Orville to go on without Wilbur? What was it like to live and work with Wilbur when he *was* alive?

For the Purposes of This Exercise

1. Examine stories you know, and make a list of the characters already established as the leads.

For example: Emma in *Madame Bovary*, Capt. John Yossarian in *Catch-22*, Dorothy in *The Wizard of Oz*, Jo in *Little Women*, Ishmael in *Moby-Dick*, Gustav von Aschenbach in *Death in Venice*, Oliver Twist in . . . *Oliver Twist*.

In each of these cases, there is a secondary character, close to the protagonist. Make a list of these men and women, the "we're number 2, but we try harder" ones.

2. Write a scene in which the number 2 character is now the big cheese. Perhaps you are considering Melanie Wilkes from *Gone With the Wind*. A perennial wallflower, in your spin she is every bit as aggressive and shrewd as Scarlett. What a shock for everyone! Melanie pushes Scarlett *well away* from her man, Mr. Ashley spineless-Wilkes, Melanie drives a newborn baby across enemy lines, out of a burning Atlanta.

Play with this. See what happens when you put power into a secondary character's hands. Is there a chance that it belonged there in the first place?

3. Now let's take a piece of your own writing and work with it. Move around the chess pieces, shake up the dice.

Select a story you're working on right now. Identify the lead character and politely walk him or her off to one side. Extend a hand to number 2 and pull them out onto center stage. Rewrite some scenes with him or her as the star, as lead. How does this sound? Is this an interesting approach? Does it have any merit? Has it made you look at your characters, and indeed the whole darn piece, in a different light? Had you been writing, unintentionally, about the "wrong brother"?

ONE LAST THOUGHT: This thing we do, this hard thing we do, is part of a long and, I believe, noble profession. The desire to write, to record and reflect and create, didn't just miraculously pop up five hundred years ago. Thousands of years ago, early men and women drew on cave walls, chronicling their lives. Now we have *People* magazine and computer "chat rooms" and paperback books that come out only after the movie. We are still trying to comment on the experience of being human and being alive.

I'm not kidding you when I confess that every single time I pick up a pen and start to write on a piece of paper, my world grinds to a millisecond halt and I am linked—no, *joined*—to my writing ancestors. Writing *matters*. Writing is important. I respect you so much for trying to make yourself a better writer.

It is astonishingly easy to turn on a computer. It takes effort and determination and a belief in yourself and a fierce and relentless awareness of the big picture of your life with YOU right smack in the middle of it all—to be a prolific and productive writer.

Good luck and keep at that cave wall.

Plot, Plot, Fizz, Fizz

This is a quickie. This exercise can be done as a warm-up for five minutes to get your mind going OR it can be done all by itself on a day when you want to write but you don't want to think.

Here we are again . . . estimating the number of plots there are in the world. One camp says there are two, another insists there are eleven, the woman who serves coffee at the Starbuck's on Seventy-fourth and Third Avenue is certain that there are two hundred plots, no more, no less, and she will give you her list of them all for fourteen dollars.

Whatever the resolution, it is an intriguing question. The moment you begin to entertain the possibility that there exists a set number of plots, you also begin to examine all the stories you know and play with the notion of *where do they fit?* Is *A Tale of Two Cities* an example of plot 2, or plot 47? What about *Flipper?* Or *Beowolf?*

I think that the "plot conundrum" compels us so because we are an organizational species, we like to arrange things into groups, we like to know the order of things. To classify and categorize things makes us feel more in control.

For the Purposes of This Exercise

Let's say that there are two plots in the world, two master plots, and that these two "*uber*" plots have born forth, from their clean and classic composition, all others. These two plots are:

1. Hero takes a journey.
2. Stranger comes to town.

Let's examine a few well-known stories and see which plot fits:

Jaws (book and movie): Well, that would be number 2, the stranger being the shark. But it is also a little bit of number 1, as the hero, Brody, does go on a personal journey.

Washington Square (book, ultimately also a movie, and also eventually a play): This is a clear-cut case of number 1. But it also has a touch of number 2.

Gone With the Wind (book and movie): This is number 1, as Scarlett O'Hara takes a long and exciting personal and physical journey.

The Cat in the Hat (book): Stranger comes to town, most definitely. That cat gave me terrific anxiety as a child . . . he stirred up such a tornado of chaotic confusion.

The Black Stallion (book and movie): Stranger comes to town (the horse) and hero takes a journey (the boy—as he comes into his own and rides the stallion in the challenge race).

Catch-22 (book and movie): Hero takes a journey—as Yossarian tries relentlessly to get out of the war and go home.

The Old Man and the Sea (book and movie): Hero takes a long, aquatic journey with only an ornery fish for company.

The Great Gatsby (book and movie): Hero takes a journey—as Gatsby searches for both love and a deeper meaning to his life.

Star Wars (movie): Hero, Luke Skywalker, takes a journey to a galaxy far, far away to find his destiny and reconcile with his past.

Make Way for Ducklings (book): Ducklings take a journey.

These give you an idea of how to play the game. Make a list of five stories if you are doing this exercise just to warm up. Make a list of twenty-five if this is your work for the day.

Remember, as in life, as in this *Workbook;* nothing is clear-cut or absolute, and control is an illusion. As you can see with just the examples listed above, there can be a fine line separating plots number 1 and 2. Often the hero takes a journey *because* a stranger comes to town. Or the stranger who comes to town and later takes a journey IS the hero. So keep an open mind and be flexible.

Try to have some fun with this exercise. If you come up with one or two more *"uber"* plots that you would like to throw into the mix, please do so. But try not to work with more than five; the point here is to simplify, not complicate.

ONE LAST THOUGHT: We haven't touched on this, but it is always handy to have a reference book or two around. These can help you to find a list of books by subject, author, or they can give you inspiration when you need to come up with twenty-five movie titles right away. In the Bibliography at the end of the *Workbook,* I've listed many reference books. You can't expect yourself to be a walking encyclopedia; we all need a little help now and then!

X Marks the Spot

If you have seen the movie *Poltergeist* (I slept with the lights on for three days after seeing it for the first time), you may well remember the chilling scene in which Craig T. Nelson, in the role of a successful real-estate broker and father, finally figures out the reason for the hauntings that have been plaguing his home. He lunges toward the greedy developer of the community in which they all live and shouts, accusingly, "You moved the headstones but *you didn't move the bodies!*" It seems as if the age-old adage could have saved everyone a lot of trouble: *location, location, location.* Recommendation: Try never to build a housing development directly over a large cemetery.

This exercise addresses the importance of place in its capacity to affect character. We are influenced by many, many elements of our surroundings. One big example would be the size, sound, and flavor of the place itself. Would Mother Teresa have become a nun if she had been born in Las Vegas? Would the Beatles have formed as a group if John and Ringo had been born in mainland China? Would Elvis have become Elvis if he had grown up in Finland?

For the Purposes of This Exercise

1. Pick a character, either fictional or real. Describe where they live. First the home/house itself: How long have they lived there, how big is it, how is it furnished? Does this character spend a lot of time at home, or is their place more like a hotel or pit stop? How much of them is invested in this residence? Is there a dominant style—country casual, urban modern, art deco, college frugal? What does the specific whereabouts of this person reveal about their personality?

2. Step outside the four walls. What is the street like, the town or city, the state, county, country, continent? Remember, this is the character's opinion, not yours. Try hard to keep the description in his or her voice. Does the character like the city in which he or she lives? Is the character planning to move? Is this a childhood home, an ancestral dwelling, one that will be very, very hard to abandon? Or has the character's job kept him or her moving every two years, never quite settling down in any one town, never setting down roots? How much has the character invested in the neighborhood? Does everyone know him or her, from the grocery store to the dry cleaners to the schools the kids go to, to the local dive bar? Or does the character live a more anonymous existence, keeping a low profile, trying not to be noticed?

This exercise can benefit from research, but it isn't dependent on it. Unlike "Don't Know Much Geography," an exercise also relating to location, this drill focuses more on *person* than *place*. Meaning that it's not so much what New Orleans really looks or sounds or smells like, as much as how your character *feels* about New Orleans. It's not so much about where in London the Hardrock Cafe is, or what the summers in Kenya are like. Think about how a certain woman feels about living in Brazil, or Austria, or Detroit. For this exercise, investigate the emotional site.

This exercise is another opportunity to work on the voice of many different characters. It will soon become obvious if *all* your characters speak in a similar voice, and if that is indeed *your* voice. Variety is good in life, and it is imperative in fiction: Although I'm sure that you are a fascinating person, I don't want to read story after story in which all the characters sound and act and think the same—the same as you. Starting with location, this is a step toward developing really diverse and distinctive characters in your writing.

The concept of character "voice" is a complex one. Your characters have experiences, and those experiences shape their personalities. But they are also born with a genetic predisposition to certain traits, as are we all. The "voice" of a character is the combination of genetic predisposition + life experience + present influences. Location is a powerful influence on character. Imagine the course of your last few weeks if, rather than having spent them where you did, you were in prison, in a hospital, in a one-room apartment with four other people. When building the details in a character's life, don't underestimate the potency of place.

Also, remember that it's possible to be a hero in the kitchen and a coward on the corner. We often change our entire opinion about the world and how it treats us depending on how safe and secure we feel. Is your character very bold in her neighborhood but a nervous wreck across county lines? Experiment with the effect LOCATION has on a character's need for self-protection. Do they need a drink immediately on arriving in a restaurant? Do they chain-smoke at home but not at work? Do they need a collection of talismen to feel safe on an airplane?

How does place affect personality?

The Rewrite Rut, or "My Name's Russell and I'm a Perfectionist"

It's way past your bedtime. You've watched *I Love Lucy, Charlie's Angels, Starsky and Hutch, Taxi, Rhoda,* and you're settling in for the 4:00 A.M. showing of *The Godfather* trilogy. You can't sleep.

You play the lines of your story over and over in your head. You think about the love scene. The flashback/fight/friend passages. None of the scenes sound right. You want to throw it all out and start again. You are approaching . . . the Rewrite Zone.

Mind you, this doesn't always play itself out at predawn. It could be pre-Oprah, or postdinnertime. There are hundreds of opportunities during your day to obsess about your work, its flaws, and its blatant need for correcting. Sometimes this fierce reflection, this literary autopsy, has behind it a stronger urge than did the desire to write it down in the first place!

How can this *be*? How could it feel better and more satisfying to *revise* than it did to *create*? Could it be that some people live to TWEAK?

Yes, it could be just that.

I took a screenwriting class in graduate school with a very pleasant young man, let's call him "Rewrite Russell." He wrote a first draft of a screenplay in 1987, during our first semester. It was a genuinely funny, commercial idea. As best as I can understand, he spent the next SIX years doing draft after draft after draft after draft. . . .

I ran into him in Los Angeles in 1994. He was trying to get some meetings with what was by then a decidedly unfunny, not charming, too choppy, and very convoluted script. In the interim he had written nothing new. "I have a lot of ideas," Russell told me, "but I just want to put this baby to bed." I didn't have the heart to tell him that his "baby" was a sophomore in high school.

Question: What's going on here? What's the purpose of this deep-seated, human inability to leave well enough alone? Why do we fuss and fidget and fret?

Answer: Because it feels safer to fiddle endlessly with a project at home than it does to pack it up and send it out into the world, to be judged on the merits, potentially to be critiqued, potentially to be ripped apart.

Question: If I submit my work to a publisher/movie studio/agent/director, etc., will it still be mine?

Answer: Yes and no. It will always come from you; you will always be the source, the parent. But as your project passes into other hands and into the dominion of publishers, or editors, or reviewers, or producers, we gradually lose control. This is not necessarily a bad thing, but it feels bad.

It's hard to let go and move on.
It's hard in relationships.
It's hard in work.
It's hard in writing.

But imagine if Jane Austen had spent a lifetime getting *one* character from *one* story perfect? Imagine if Shakespeare rewrote *Romeo and Juliet* for fifty years? Imagine how much less wonderful our world would be if Charles Dickens and Charles Bukowski, or Tennyson and W. H. Auden, or Ben Franklin and Aretha Franklin had worked on being perfect, not prolific?

Do your BEST DRAFT and move on.

The Stuff That Dreams Are Made Of

Falling and flying: These are the two main themes that appeared in my childhood dreams. Also: not knowing my lines for the class play (and the curtain's going up), not having studied for the exam about to begin, and suddenly becoming aware that I have no clothes on in a very public place. Anxiety dreams? I think yes.

Ask people if they remember their dreams and you will most likely get an emphatic answer: No, never ever, or Yes, I always do. Dream "forgetters" usually insist that they just *don't* dream, at all, so there's nothing *to* remember. Dream "rememberers" find great meaning in the symbols and icons planted in their dreams, and tend to assume that you will find the waking excavation equally as fascinating as do they.

Where, oh where, is the middle ground?

In ancient civilizations, dreams were taken very seriously. To dream about your foot falling off might foretell four years of bad harvest. Dream about birds and your spouse is cheating on you. Dream about gold and you'll be destitute in twelve months.

It's doubtful now whether or not the majority of Americans set much store by their dreams. With the advent of Freudian analysis and its incorporation into the vernacular, we tend to automatically assign psychoanalytic meaning to our dreams and their clues. A cigar becomes a phallic object; a train going into or out of a tunnel becomes a phallic reference; a dream about skyscrapers is evidence of penis envy. Is this true? When I dream about a rainstorm in my living room, am I subconsciously voicing an unexpressed sadness trapped in my body?

I'm sure that you've heard tell of the experiments done on

sleep deprivation. While I believe that these were done in a systematic way by our government to observe the behavior of astronauts forced to stay awake for days at a time, just ask any mother of a newborn baby. Sleep deprivation sucks, and it can make you CRAZY. After twenty-four hours we start feeling cranky and fuzzy and wired. After forty-eight hours our judgment is seriously impaired, and we exhibit personality distortions. After three days, we are a babbling, hallucinating, stumbling *mess*. We see things. We hear voices. We make no sense when we speak.

What the scientists found out was this: If the brain is not given its preferred outlet for the inevitable psychic overload that occurs on a daily basis, then it will take any port in a storm. The dreams will occur anyway, only we are awake. We will walk around thinking we see little wings sprouting from the heads of the check-out clerks at the supermarket. Our parents start to resemble Rabbit and Tigger from Winnie the Pooh. Our bedroom suddenly hosts a river, running under the bed and into the closet. And it all seems real.

Dreams are not just fluffy pink clouds to rest on in between dinner and breakfast. We *must* dream. All the stuff that happens to us during the day—our thoughts, our behaviors, our experiences—these are all worked out and digested and revisited during our downtime. Our nightly pit stop. Deprive sleep and you deprive dreaming. Deprive dreaming and you have a fry-ball on your hands, just this close to going over the edge.

Now, down to business. This is not a one-shot, one-afternoon exercise. This will take you at least one week to complete. It could take a year. Work on this exercise while you are working on the others. Write your dreams down as often as you can remember to do so; over time, this ongoing project will begin to affect the other writing you are doing concurrently. Perhaps an element from last Wednesday's dream will find its way into your "Don't Know Much Geography" or the "Character Pages" exercise. You might possibly dream an entire story; beginning, middle, and end. It can happen.

For the Purposes of This Exercise

1. Write down the dreams you remember most vividly. Go as far back as you can recall. Put down as much detail as you can dredge up, and try to give each dream a title: for example, Aunt Winnie Turns into the Moon.

2. Get into the habit of writing your dreams down shortly after waking up; you might want to keep paper and pencil next to your bed. Try this for a week or two. See if your recall improves with practice; can you summon back more details, any peculiar features, who was in your dream and what was their function? Was this a scary dream? Are your dreams frequently menacing?

You will find that, with practice, you'll become proficient at recording your dreams. Right upon waking up, you'll reach across the nearby table and grab your pad and pen. You write furiously. Once you've transcribed your dream, you shower and dress and go on with your day. By midmorning, you've forgotten what the dream was about. But no worry! You wrote it down.

3. Think of a book or a movie that had a dream sequence in it. Write down the author and title, and then describe the dream as best as you can. Did this device work? Was it really necessary to further the plot? Was it a distraction; did it take you out of the story? Dream sequences in fiction are not unlike the little girl with a little curl right in the middle of her forehead: When they work, they really work, and when they don't, they can stink up the whole story.

Think about the purpose of putting a dream in a story. List as many reasons as you can come up with for using a dream, and as many as you can come up with against. Which side is longer? Which side is more compelling?

In regard to writing, dreams resemble telephone calls. If your character has to leave whatever he or she is doing or is about to take a phone call, it had better be for a good reason. The importance of the information being conveyed in the dream, or telephone call, had better outweigh the chance that your readers will feel cheated and distracted.

If you are working on a story at present, you might try including a dream or dream-related event in your plot. Remember, this is just an exercise and it certainly need not remain in your final draft. Experiment. Explore the possibility: Your lead character has a dream. About what? What happens to her and her circle of influence after this dream? Does it convey a secret? Does it reveal suppressed information? Does it disclose knowledge that we, the reader, have always been aware of?

ONE LAST THOUGHT: It's tempting and titillating and seductive to solve dream riddles by assigning definitive meanings to symbols from our sleep. However, sometimes, as Freud said, *"A cigar is just a cigar."*

End Well

Here's the thing—I don't want to die. Even during the worst, worst, most unendurable times, the most depressing "How did I ever sink so low?" moments, I have not wanted to end my life. That's just me.

I've always wanted one more day. One more meal. One more cup of hot, fresh coffee, one more listen to a good Delta Blues song, one more George Clooney movie, one more look at an amazing, beautiful, tortured Van Gogh painting of a tree. One more—whatever. *More.* I don't want this to end, ever. They will have to drag me off to the great beyond kicking and screaming. Dignity in death? Someone else's story.

Let's focus on the Big D: Death. The Dark Beyond. The Last Breath. We will one day *cease to be.* Our tender wet hearts will stop beating. No more air or blood or disease or pain. Our friends and family gather together and grieve and then, eventually, their lives go on. Seems sad and depressing?

Endings *are* sad. Freud said, *"End well,"* and it takes some living to really *get* what he meant. Without meaning to sound simplistic, I believe that life is made up of a series of journeys. We open a door and go on a ways, see what's there, and then sometimes we decide to keep going on in this new direction and sometimes we go back to the turning-off point and return to the way we were heading before. Best as we can remember. Endings and beginnings. Opening and closing doors. Starting and stopping.

We don't talk much about death in our culture. In some ways, it is a taboo subject. Not exactly cocktail conversation. I'll have a vodka martini, Boodles gin *very* dry with three olives, and by the way, are you planning to be buried or cremated?

If you choose to write as your main activity, some characters in your stories might eventually die. Maybe lots of your characters will die. Maybe you will devote your life to writing about sick and dying people. Or maybe you'll write about hamsters, hamsters that die. Cloth hamsters. Stone hamsters. But that's not too likely.

For the Purposes of This Exercise

1. Write about the experiences you have had with death. Try to draw this part of the exercise out for a few days, writing one experience at a time. Don't race through it. Write about each experience fully: Describe the person who died and your relationship with them. Write about your experience of their death: Were they ill, did they linger, was there an accident, did they die at home or in a hospital? Describe how their death made you feel: right after, months later, years later. Did you go to the funeral? Did you see their dead body? Did it frighten you? Have you been to the grave since the funeral? Were they cremated? Where are the ashes? Did they leave specific wishes for their burial/funeral/memorial? Did they write a will or a living will? Was it adhered to? Was their death a sad experience for you, or was it something else? Explain.

There is the possibility that the only "death experience" you have had so far is the demise of a pet or a nondomesticated animal of whom you were fond. Write about that. A loss is a loss.

After you've done at least two examples for question 1, move on to:

2. The next part of this exercise requires you to think back very carefully over movies you have seen and books you have read. It can also include plays, operas, and puppet shows, basically any complete *story* in which a character dies. Is it the Wicked Witch in *Oz*? Is it the Debra Winger character in *Terms of Endearment*?

Write down the title of the work, and name the character who dies. Then, in detail, describe the death. What did they die from? How did it affect you? Do you think it *worked* as a cinematic/literary device? Was it sad? Was it meant to be sad? Did you cry? Did it seem genuine, honest—or was it manipulative . . . a "tearjerker"? Was it predictable? If *you* were to rewrite or refilm that scene (or group of scenes), would you make changes?

If possible, do at least five of these analyses. Begin to consider this question: In storytelling, are there basic categories into which death scenes fall? Can you identify any groupings or divisions? Of the death scenes you have described, are there any similarities?

Do you sense that the writer was trying to write a death scene for its own sake, rather than allowing the death of that particular character to happen or NOT to happen in its own organic place in the story?

Are there overall stylistic "death landmarks" that need to be placed in a story when writing a death scene? Do you feel that all lives are different, but all deaths have the same sad face? Or are our deaths as unique and individual as were our lives?

3. Create a death scene. It is not a terrible idea to practice writing about death. It may *feel* weird—as if we are inviting in an unwelcome guest. Will death be less likely to pay us a visit if we never, ever, ever talk about it? If we never, ever, ever talk about death, will it feel unwelcome and therefore, perhaps insulted, *staying away* until the last possible moment?

If you are a very superstitious person, this exercise will be hard for you. Writing about something with as many emotional repercussions as death is a tough assignment. I recommend that if it makes you feel very uncomfortable to do this, that you not push it. When you are ready, it will call to you. Until then, don't forget those cloth hamsters.

If you feel up to it . . . let's proceed.

Use this as a forum to practice writing a death scene. This does not mean that I am suggesting that you write the death scene of someone you love, as a cathartic means to overcome frustration and irritation. This is a writing exercise, NOT a psychotherapeutic drill. In order to get the most out of this exercise, pick a scenario with which you would like to experiment. This might be an illness, an accident, or the end of a long life.

I do not recommend that you write about people in your own life. Rather, I recommend that you create characters for this exercise. Perhaps you might like to use characters from a story you are working on, or a character from a story you have already written.

At the top of the page, describe the situation in one brief sentence. Outline the characters involved, and the physical setting. Then set your watch for thirty minutes and get down to it.

Be prepared: Writing about death is not easy. It can bring up feelings that are painful and difficult. After these exercises, I strongly recommend that you record your reactions in your journal. It may or may not be emotionally disconcerting. My hope for you, as a writer, is that this exercise enables you to explore a difficult but potentially rewarding area.

ONE VERY, VERY, LAST THOUGHT: A few years after our mother's death, my sister tried out for an acting/directing workshop in New York City. There was a long application form to fill out. Two of the questions were:

1. Mother's address
2. Mother's occupation

My sister thought for a moment, then wrote down:

1. Deadland
2. Being dead

This has always struck me as being fantastically honest and funny. It's not easy to be funny about your mother's death. It's not really considered in very good taste to be funny about your mother's death. In our culture it is acceptable to be grim and subdued where death is concerned. So . . . perhaps this exercise *might* provide an opportunity to consider death in a more wild, loose, unfamiliar light.

Deadland? Lifeland? Whoknowsland.

Lost and Found

Hunger. Appetite. Craving. Desire.

We are a voracious species. Whether we are opening Pandora's box, killing the cat, or coveting our neighbor's cow (or wife), we have both eyes wide open and we are on the prowl.

Some things we need a little, some a lot. Some things are purely physical, like a need for water or air. Some are intangible, like the hunger for love and respect. Whatever the specifics, we step right up on a daily basis and tell Santa what we want.

What happens when we put aside our simple needs? Not that desires for lunch and a warm bed are insignificant, but let's raise the stakes. There are needs that go much deeper. Some of us have wanted something so much for so long that we are no longer able to separate the passion from the person: We *become* the longing; it fills us up. We wake up thinking about it. We go to bed planning a fresh assault for tomorrow. Our soul has merged with the hunger and we are now one big voracious "want."

For the Purposes of This Exercise

1. Start with yourself. Think of something—an object, a person, an intangible challenge or tangible reward—that you could see yourself making a long-term play for. If you have ever been or are still involved in a personal quest, describe it. What is it about this thing/person/reward that makes a long and frustrating struggle seem worthwhile? Go into as much detail as you can. When did you first realize you wanted "X"? Do you know anyone else who also wants it? Have you ever gotten close to getting it? Do you really want to get it, or is the pursuit part of the pleasure? Where do you or did you have to go to find this cherished thing or person or place?

Perhaps you know a person who is on such a crusade. What is it they're seeking? Think up as many examples as you can of things we chase after.

2. After you have come up with a list, the exercise becomes an examination of the type of person who would launch themselves on such a potentially discouraging life's effort. What kind of person sets their sights so high that there is a good chance that they will *never* achieve, *never* find, *never* hold in their hands the object of their obsession? A fascinating dilemma.

Write in as much depth as you can about the feelings you associate with such an all-consuming quest. Imagine it first for yourself, then for people you know or know of who are on quests, then try to create a character who is on a life-long pilgrimage. Do they feel a little unbalanced, obsessed? Is the longing and yearning reflected in their every step and action? Is this person aware of the fact that not everyone else is as single-minded as they are? Do they feel the distance between themselves and the rest of "normal" society? Or do they feel themselves to be normal and the rest of the world to be tepid?

Has the person in question, the "searcher," chosen this quest *because* it is impossible to realize? Is part of the appeal the very fact that it is forbidden, taboo, and incredibly hard to attain?

Could they be more comfortable in the search than they are in the objective itself?

Is this search one of retaliation? For example, after a loved one dies of cancer, has your character set out to personally find the cure, blinded by the pain and anger of his or her loss? There are obviously many variations on this theme. In days of knights and round tables and impossible swords, some men went off on quests because, in truth, there wasn't much else for them to do. Does the quest you are describing define the person, or does the person define the quest?

Furthermore, what is it that makes the "having" of this thing an impossibility? Is it their "station" in life? Their age? Socio-economic status? Are they not smart enough, brave enough, pretty or handsome enough? Successful enough? Is the lack a reality or a figment of the searcher's insecure mind? Do you imagine they will be triumphant? Or will they be eaten by a proverbial dragon?

3. Now that you have some experience writing about things we quest for and how the quest feels, consider the crusades made popular in the stories we all know. What was Scarlett O'Hara's driving passion? What were Hansel and Gretel looking for? How about Joan of Arc? Describe some quests from the books, movies, and plays of your experience. Consider the crusaders within your own world. Do you have a friend or family member who has spent a lifetime single-mindedly pursuing a dream to the exclusion of a so-called balanced life?

Remember: Desire can guide, but it can also demolish. It is not rational. It is intense.

It is in you.

What can you see yourself still desiring twenty-five years from now?

Bad Appetites

There is a now-famous, apocryphal story regarding the early career of the boxer Mike Tyson—perhaps you already know it.

Tyson was a teenager, a fighting *machine,* coiled rage in the ring. Seems the fellow who would come to be his trainer (and his adoptive father) had come to watch Tyson box and, after witnessing his astonishing strength and fierce concentration, turned to the person next to him and said, *"He hits with BAD INTENTIONS."*

There is a hunger inside of every living body. As we grow and become aware of the world as being both separate from us *and* not existing simply to serve our needs, we begin a lifelong search for relief.

In an attempt to tolerate life's frustrations, we search for relief. Some people smoke three packs of cigarettes a day, some drink, others gamble, use drugs, sex, exercise maniacally. Some eat. Some don't eat. Some people need a hot bath, herbal tea, and a book. We all need outlets for our frustrations and anxieties. Some will be constructive; some will be destructive.

Mike Tyson invested each punch with the anger and resentment and intense emotion he kept inside. His boxing was a release. His boxing was a statement of self. This is not an endorsement of boxing as a means to calm your inner demons. But I do recognize that human beings are powerful and passionate, capable of emphatic—and sometimes extreme—feelings. What we do with those feelings says a great deal about who we are. It also makes for good storytelling.

For the Purposes of This Exercise

1. Consider the ways in which people deal with their demons, and ask yourself how those particular choices will affect a person's behavior, short- and long-term.

For instance: George has always been told that he is handsome, but stupid. He will never get into Harvard, and his father refuses to pay for a "lesser" school. George is pressed into marrying well, working in a menial, boring job, and accepting his limited abilities. He does just that: He marries a rich and spoiled heiress, he works for her father, and carries inside of him a growing bitterness and rage. At the age of forty-five, George's father dies. Here at last is release—right? The noose of oppression is now untied?

Now, here is the absolutely fascinating thing about human behavior. The death of George's father sends him into a tailspin. Rather than freeing him, he plunges into a deep depression. He begins drinking heavily. He slacks off at work. He cheats on his wife. For several years, he becomes totally unhinged. WHY?

Because change ain't easy. George's father totally defined him. George lived his life by his father's rules. When his dad died, he didn't know who he *was* anymore. He could no longer say to himself, "I'm a person oppressed and misunderstood and ruined by his father." He would have to change it to ". . . by his DEAD father," and even to someone as stepped on as George, that sounded lame. He realized intellectually that it was his chance now to be his own person. But after forty-five years of blaming his father for who he was, George wasn't sure who "his own person" WAS.

George made choices to cope with the anger he felt toward his father's poor opinion of him. Those choices shaped his behavior and, over time, his identity.

Start with people you know—real or fictional characters. First, identify the choices made: How did Person A deal with the challenges presented to them? Did they run and hide or face the music? Did they turn the volume up or down? How high a price were they prepared to pay for inner peace? How did Person A's decisions affect their ability to successfully handle their life? What were the consequences?

This exercise asks you to do some deep investigating into the complex, complicated—and deeply flawed—human soul. The stuff you'll be working on here is the material you'll use in future stories and characters and plots and situations.

People have many layers, many facets. As a writer, what will you show, what will you hide, what will you imply?

2. One surefire way to root out our demons is to present moral people with a choice and then examine the road not taken. For instance, your mother is a terrible cook. She has made terrible meals for you your entire life. The day comes for you to plan your wedding, and, her heart rumbling with maternal love, your mom announces her plan to cook the wedding meal. What to do? Do you explode and tell her you'd rather serve up dog food? Or do you swallow hard, smile, and thank her for her kind thought?

Make a list of at least five people, fictional or real, known to be honorable and virtuous. Then set up a few situations in which their upstanding and decent natures are well tested. Give them opportunities to steal, lie, cheat, betray, deceive, abandon. Let them do the right thing, and then ask them how they really feel. Did they have a longing to lash out? Did they have a hankering to cause harm?

And what if your Andy Hardy/Pollyanna character does cross the line? It makes great reading when a noble soul descends to the depths. Examine a few situations in which a supposedly "good" man or woman is presented with a test of their scruples . . . and fails.

For example: A small-town policeman is left in charge of a cache of stolen money and jewels. It is up to him to record the loot into the police ledger. Who will know if he skims a little off the top to pay for his wife's operation? Who will suffer if a diamond ring or a ruby and sapphire necklace goes home in his jacket pocket to finance his kids' education? He's worked his whole life for poor wages, with long hours and the constant threat of personal injury. Is it ever justifiable to do something wrong for the right reason?

These dilemmas make for absorbing and intriguing storytelling.

3. Evil characters are fascinating in and of themselves, but much more compelling are bad boys and girls who harbor the capacity to do right. Make a list of at least five naughty people, fictional or real. Put them in a situation in which they have a clear opportunity to do wrong, and let a moment of principle wash over them.

For example: A notorious drug dealer is faced with the daughter of a longtime friend, asking to buy a dime bag of heroin. How easy would it be for the dealer to take the money and start another young user on their way! But no—the "bad guy" struggles with his conscience and refuses to sell the friend's child the heroin. The dealer sits the girl down and lectures her, as best as he can. Do you want this life? Do you want to really *see* where this will take you? The dealer spends an afternoon with the young girl, showing her around the drug-infested neighborhood in which he deals. The girl goes home shaken. Why does the dealer do this? He might not be sure himself. But inside a dark heart rests a tiny, grim light. If—as a writer—you can expose that, you will create fascinating characters.

Bad appetites make for good stories.

The Committee,
or
Bad Guys: 65/Good Guys: 1

When I was thirteen years old, for reasons known still best to herself, my mother printed up twenty-five T-shirts saying THE CAROLINE SHARP BORING SHOW and one saying just CAROLINE SHARP. That Christmas, all of our family and friends got "Boring Show" T-shirts. I got the one with just my name on it . . . in case, I guess, someone really needed to know who the boring person was. She had an odd sense of humor.

I tell this story not for sorrow's sake, although God only knows I put all my therapist's children through college trying to make some sense out of this and other cruelties of my childhood, but to suggest this: You never know when something is going to happen to you that will profoundly affect your self-confidence. My mother was—she *thought*—poking fun at my preteen shyness and frequent inability to tell stories quickly and to the point. I often stuttered and rambled. Now, as an adult, I am very self-conscious of being boring. Wonder why.

There are people who don't doubt themselves. Maybe three or four in the whole world, but they do exist. Everyone else, however, has some misgivings, concerns, questions. We are a little bit nervous all the time.

A lack of confidence can hold you back. If you don't believe in yourself, it is hard to suppose that anyone else will either. Every time you put yourself out there, you hear past laughter and humiliation in your head. You're stuck in a rut of shame and embarrassment: you can't do it, you're a loser, you'll always be a loser, who are you trying to kid? Those voices, however *old* they are, can cut to the heart. They are the voices of your Committee. They never sleep. They live to plant the seeds of self-doubt in your heart and anxiety in your brain.

Here's a thought: Your Committee, the loud and persistent panel of your worst critics that has been living in your head since you tripped and fell at the seventh-grade dance, accidently farting on the way down, is there with your permission. You are the Landlord. How about *that*? These horrible thoughts, once upon a time a gift from someone else, have become your own. You repeat them to yourself as if they were Gospel.

NEWSFLASH: My mother wasn't right. Chances are, yours wasn't either. All the horrible stuff about yourself you carry around like the Eleventh Commandment, like incontrovertible fact, is no more than one person's opinion. People can be wrong. We used to believe that the world was flat. We were stone certain that the sun revolved around the Earth. We were without hesitation positive that grapefruit juice did "dissolve fat." They could be all wrong about YOU, too.

I read somewhere that it takes sixty-five good things to wipe out the damage done by hearing *one* bad thing about ourselves. This sounds right. We agree when someone says we're stupid and question the fool who says we're smart. If you think I'm a dunce you must really, deeply know me. But if you say I have talent— well, what do *you* know?

You're on your way home from winning the Nobel Prize, and some kid shouts out, "Mommy, that lady's face is *weird!*" Years of therapy later . . .

There is no easy way out of this one. Self-doubt plagues all the artistic people I know. Inasmuch as writers are people who think deeply, who consider themselves, the world, the meaning of life, and the purpose of it all, they are also going to be people who can be wounded deeply. Yes, you are the Landlord, yes, you can insist that the Committee MOVE OUT. But it can take a long time to really *feel* different, to really believe in yourself. Sometimes you have to fake it a little first—*pretend* that you believe in your talent. *Pretend* that you believe you can write. Invent yourself as a writer, then do the writing. In time, the authenticity will catch up to the invention.

"Dear John . . ."

Do people write letters anymore? I know they talk on the telephone, a *great deal,* and they send faxes and E-mail. Our means of communications are swift and disposable. We don't wait for much of anything these days. Images on television and movies are measured in "IPS" units: "images per *second.*" Terrifying. Our minds are used to receiving information at a pace that would have stunned our ancestors into a brain-freezing stupor. We are faster, but are we any better?

Set the clock back 110 years. You live in a town near Boston, say Springfield, and you have a relative in a town near New York City, say Bedford. You're in Springfield; she's in Bedford. It's 1889.

You see each other once a year at a holiday gathering. To reach this party spot, both of you have to put in about two days' worth of traveling. You'll stay at the home of your mother's sister for five days—really the bare minimum to warrant the effort of packing and planning and travel. You'll bring a trunk, one or two cloth bags, a hatbox, a shoe box, a train case with your basic toiletries, and perhaps a basket or two or three with various fresh food items as an offering to your host and hostess.

In preparation for this trip, you will most likely have spent six months writing letters back and forth to your Bedford cousin. Each letter would have been the product of an afternoon's thought and execution. Each letter would have taken at least a week to arrive. Your cousin would then have returned the correspondence. Two letters each a month. Two chances *per month* to say something to each other. Think about it. Think about how often you speak to your friends and family. Imagine if you had only one or two chances a month to converse. Would you plan carefully? Would you verbally economize and purposefully express yourself? I believe you would.

The Bedford-Springfield reunion is, of course, completely imaginary. However, while the specifics are made up, the circumstances are not. The ease with which we travel these days is a recent change. We can move our bodies rapidly by car or plane. We move our thoughts rapidly by telephone or fax or computer. To sit still, to sit in a chair and read, to be still with ourselves and contemplate the racing world around us—this kind of inactivity has been redefined as lazy and apathetic.

As the pace of life has sped up around us, it has become increasingly difficult to do anything slowly without running the risk of being branded sluggish or lethargic. I see this as a dangerous assumption. As we focus more and more on the speed with which something can be done and the importance of the result over the process, we become less and less a reflective people and more and more a superficial, shallow, cosmetic people. We are more concerned with style than with substance.

I believe that it is our ability to delay gratification, in all its many forms, that defines us as adults. Can we wait for our reward? Can we bear discomfort? It is very difficult to postpone pleasure and relief. We are teased with suggestions of pleasure on every corner: liquor ads, cigarette ads, fancy cars and airplane travel and hotels and casinos and clothes and jewels. Relief is right out there, dangled in front of our faces like the proverbial carrot to the proverbial donkey.

Working toward our due isn't the message anymore: It's all in the having, not in the wanting.

For the Purposes of This Exercise

Hit the "pause" button for a moment. Let's pretend you don't have a telephone. Or a computer. Or a Federal Express drop-off station around the block, or a fax machine ... OR ANY-THING ... except a piece of paper and your pen. In order to communicate with people who are not living in your immediate environs, you must write to them.

1. Pick a person you care about. Start with a real person, preferably living. Write them a letter, at least one long page. Don't type this letter! It's important that you handwrite it, touch pen or pencil to paper, in a manner similar to your ancestors. Tell them about yourself, your life, your friends, and your family. Be chatty, informative. Share the news. Take your time. If you're feeling frisky, try writing a letter from you to a famous, historical person. What would you tell about yourself and your life to Albert Einstein? Marie Curie? Julius Caesar? What might they write back to you?

2. Think of two fictional characters, or two celebrities, or two famous cultural icons, such as a politician or an actress. They may or may not be from the same "story." Write a letter from one to the other and then return the correspondence.

For instance: What if Queen Victoria knew Marilyn Monroe? What would they write to each other about? How about Vincent Van Gogh and Pablo Picasso? Or, more current, how about Frasier and Jerry Seinfeld? Rhett Butler and Alfred the butler? Andy Warhol and one of the Hanson Brothers?

Pick a book or movie with which you are very familiar. In the voice of a character from that story—say, the Demi Moore character from *Ghost* or Bridget Jones from *Bridget Jones' Diary*—write a letter. Let your imagination fly; they can be writing to someone from their world, or to someone completely of your own spin. The one rule is that you must stay true to their already established personality.

3. If it is kept, a letter can be a permanent record of a time and phase of your life, chronicled on paper for you to reread in years to come. Perhaps there were letters you wrote but did not send, letters you wrote but ripped up and threw out, letters you thought through to the last word but never realized. Take some time here to revisit some of your life's dramatic moments. Remember what was happening, and who was involved. On a piece of paper, sketch down what you recall: who were the key players and what was the event in question. Then write a letter to one or

more of the featured people in this incident. Try to evoke the feelings, the intensity of that hour. You may find a powerful detail for your next story in the shadow of your own memories.

For example: Your brother was a star athlete. He excelled at every sport; he was better than you at everything. Then the summer you turned twelve, you outshined him at swimming. You practiced and practiced and finally beat him in a swim meet, in front of everyone. Even though he shook your hand and seemed not to care at all, you sensed that something had changed between you. Later that night, you watched out of your bedroom window as your brother, in a rage, threw out all of his swimming trophies. You never told him that you saw him do this. Your brother never swam competitively again.

Write your brother a letter. You are twelve, and you are disappointed in him for not being able to make any room in his world for you to be good at something, too. You are twelve, and you have come to realize that your perfect brother is flawed and imperfect and you still love him. You wonder if he loves you. Letters afford us the opportunity to think about what we are going to say before we say it. We can express our thoughts at leisure, eloquently, keenly, carefully.

Who knows . . . if you don't already, you might come away from this exercise with a desire to write letters!

7-Up

In the early 1960s, the British cinematographer Michael Apted started a long-term documentary called *7-Up*. He interviewed a small group of children, all aged seven, asking them questions about themselves, their opinions on life, and their hopes for the future. Every seven years after that, he found each of these same people and reinterviewed them, asking some of the same questions and some new ones. The results were fascinating; certain aspects of personality changed radically with life experience, while some others remained constant throughout. At last count, the subjects of *7-Up* were in their late thirties and due to be reinterviewed when they turned forty-two.

If you look back over the span of your own life, you probably can find certain traits that have changed and perhaps disappeared with maturation. I know for a fact that my kindergarten report card held clues to many difficulties I was to encounter: "Caroline is an enthusiastic girl, easily frustrated, quick to learn." Not much has changed.

This exercise will examine the impact of age on a character's judgment, subjective beliefs, and actual abilities. For instance: You are in a car accident in which the driver is killed but you escape unharmed. What would your emotional reaction to this be if you were five years old? Fifteen years old? Forty years old? Below are listed a selection of scenarios from which to start. You're encouraged to come up with your own as well.

For each exercise, I recommend that you pick two ages: Examine the scenario you establish from the standpoint of these two different time periods. These need not be ages about which you have personal experience, but they can be. You can write from your own point of view or from that of a fictional character.

You also have the choice of using a character from your own imagination or one created by someone else.

Spend at least fifteen minutes on each age—exploring the impact that age-specific perception will have on a character's feelings and actions. How might falling in love affect a sixteen year old versus a sixty year old? How about losing a job? Being diagnosed with terminal cancer? Allow yourself to dive into the realm of that age, walk around in it, remember or imagine the colors, smells, sounds that affect you.

This is not an easy exercise, but it will give you good practice at stretching beyond your own present situation, hopefully allowing you to add depth and honesty to your work.

Possible situations:

The loss of a parent or grandparent.
A new job.
Losing one's hair as a bad side effect to medication.
Being in a near-fatal airplane crash.
Winning a singing contest.
Learning to drive stick shift.
Rescuing someone in physical peril.
Telling a lie and getting caught.
Teaching someone to make an omelet.
Telling a friend that you don't like his or her spouse.
Using dishonest and deceitful means to get a promotion.
Giving someone in need money, anonymously.
Breaking a china object that is someone's cherished possession.
Kissing a stranger.
Being mugged.
Memorizing a long poem.
Reading someone else's letters.
Getting arrested for driving under the influence.
Saving up to buy a piece of jewelry for a loved one.

One Last Thought

I don't know you, but I am proud of you. In this busy, crazy, hectic world, you have made time for your writing. You have prioritized your already stretched-to-the-limit day to include at least thirty minutes of reflection, contemplation, recording. This is not easy. I really understand. Some mornings I wake up and, within minutes, I know that it's going to be a struggle to write. I don't want to sit with myself; I don't want to go to the frequently painful and uncomfortable places writing takes me. But then I think about you and other writers I have had the good fortune to know and writers I admire but will never meet, and then it doesn't seem so much like a chore as a privilege.

In this day of computers and superfast information and increasingly dehumanized communication, I believe that the writer is more important to society than ever. Someone who takes the time to sit down, perhaps with pen or pencil in hand, and express themselves in their own words—this is a person with something to say and the commitment to say it. Writing takes time. Writing expresses self. Writing means something.

I sincerely hope that this *Workbook* offers you some hints and guidelines, some observations and suggestions and tools that you can take with you on the path to becoming the best writer you can be. You have a story in you that only you can tell. Don't stop trying until you have told it. Don't give up when it gets hard, because writing *is* hard. In fact, when it gets hard, double your efforts. You're getting near to the mother lode of material and the difficulty you're experiencing is a perfectly normal human reaction to avoid pain. Unfortunately, writers can't really avoid pain. We have to feel to write and in order to feel—you guessed it—

sometimes we have to feel not great stuff. But it is worth it. The writing itself makes it worthwhile.

I don't have one all-encompassing piece of advice to impart at this closing moment—wish that I did. All I know about writing, and just about everything I know about life, is already here in these pages. However, in an attempt to summarize:

1. Writing is an important thing to do.
2. A writer is a person who actually writes.
3. Writers should read a lot.
4. In order to write about your world, or your imaginary world, you'll need to experience, observe, and reflect.
5. Not necessarily in that order.

I wish you all the best, and I look forward to reading your work.

Appendix

Basic Etiquette for Reading and Responding to Your Peers' Work, or Miss Manners Comes to Your Writing Group

I have had both the fortune and the misfortune to be in several writing groups. Some of them were uplifting, encouraging, and helpful. Others were a complete waste of time, hurtful, and discouraging. What was it that made the difference?

A writing group can serve many purposes. A well-run group provides help on two major fronts: It can be a social forum for writers of varying ability to share their personal struggles with the writing life, and it can be a structured environment for writers to share their work, get feedback, encouragement, and constructive comments. If your group is composed largely of first-time members, there's a good chance that everyone will launch into their critiques with sharpened knives and rather brutal evaluations. They're relishing their new role as judge of your less-wonderful-than-their writing. However, inevitably, once the circle has gone around and everyone's felt the horror of having their work dissected and ripped to shreds, the comments tend to mellow and become much more constructive and supportive.

Are writing groups helpful? This is a subjective call. Some people find them to be essential antidotes to the isolating nature of a writer's day. Getting together, whether once a week, once a month, or once every season can help to remind us that we are not alone in tearing our hair out over the frustration of an impossible sentence. I also know many successful writers who find them to be an indulgence, a misuse of time, and a guaranteed way to dilute one's focus.

It would seem that people's opinions of, and use for, writing groups depends as much on personality as on timeliness.

However, having said all that, there is a good chance that during the course of your life as a writer, you will be asked by a peer to "give a quick read" to their work. You may be in a writing group with them. You may be on vacation together, at their house for coffee, doing laundry, at a family reunion. It happens all the time: Writers need feedback. You know what I mean. You've just finished a draft of your latest short story or a chapter of your first novel, and you need to know if it's good or if it's garbage. You need to hear how it sounds to a fresh ear. You hand your work over to Person X and then wait, hating the waiting, praying for a good review, hoping that Person X will be honest and kind.

Here are some basic guidelines for the responsible and compassionate handling of someone else's work.

1. *Be prompt:* This is very important. Few things are as awful as a nonresponse. Try to assess right away how long it will take for you to read the work in question, and then set aside that time. If this is a busy time for you, if you feel pretty sure that it'll be a struggle for you to read the work in a timely fashion, tell the writer up front. Give a realistic (*not* optimistic) estimate as to how long you'll need to read and respond. The writer then has the option of waiting for you to read their work, or thanking you for your honesty and finding someone else.

2. *Be kind:* No one really benefits from having their work destroyed. The first one hundred stories I wrote were all pretty bad. They needed to be written, as each one led to the next and the next one after that, each one a minuscule improvement over the one before. If someone had read story 75 and judged it against

the great masters, I would have been stopped cold. Remember that the person you are judging is working along a continuum, progressing step by step, story by story. Try to find one good thing for every less good one you point out. A garden grows by being watered, pruned, and nurtured—not annihilated.

3. *Critique objectively:* This is very hard. If we find a story to be terrible, it's sometimes hard to remind ourselves that our opinion is just that—*our* opinion. If we think a story about pirates is the worst thing we have ever read, there might be in our distaste a measure of our own enmity toward pirate stories in general. Try to evaluate for style and technique more than for content. It's not really helpful to tell someone that you can't stand the heroine in the story they wrote. It would be more beneficial to point to a specific overuse of adjectives or a sameness in the voice and tone of all the characters.

So, be prompt in your comments, be kind in your comments, and be specific in your comments. Read and respond to someone else's work as you would like them to read and respond to yours.

Bibliography

Section One: *To Writers by Writers*

These books on the writing craft and the writing life share one common characteristic: They are all written *by* writers. These writers have taken considerable time and effort to share their own personal observations and experiences. As with the study of any craft, you can go way overboard looking for the one magic piece of advice that will unlock the mystery and make it all easy. These books can't tell you *how to write*. They can tell you, often quite eloquently, how these people did it. There is a lot to learn here—but remember, you won't find your own true voice by rummaging around in the attic of other writers.

Brande, Dorothea. *Becoming a Writer.* New York: Tarcher/Putnam, 1934.

Dillard, Annie. *Living by Fiction.* New York: Perennial Library, Harper & Row, 1982.

Fadiman, Anne. *Ex Libris: Confessions of a Common Reader.* New York: Farrar, Straus & Giroux, 1988.

Gardner, John. *The Art of Fiction: Notes on Craft for Writers.* New York: Vintage Books, 1991.

Gardner, John. *On Becoming a Novelist.* New York: Perennial Library, Harper & Row, 1983.

Goldberg, Natalie. *Wild Mind: Living the Writer's Life.* New York: Bantam Books, 1990.

Goldberg, Natalie. *Writing Down the Bones: Freeing the Writer Within.* Boston and London: Shambhala, 1986.

Gordimer, Nadine. *Writing and Being.* Cambridge: Harvard University Press, 1995.

Lamott, Anne. *Bird by Bird: Some Instructions on Writing and Life.* New York and San Francisco: Pantheon Books, 1994.

Llosa, Mario Vargas. *A Writer's Reality.* Boston: Houghton Mifflin, 1991.

Lodge, David. *The Art of Fiction*. New York: Penguin Books, 1992.

Lodge, David. *The Practice of Writing*. New York: Penguin Press, 1997.

Rhodes, Richard. *How to Write: Advice and Reflections*. New York: William Morrow, 1995.

Sternburg, Janet. *The Writer on Her Work* (volume II). New York and London: W. W. Norton, 1991.

Ueland, Brenda. *If You Want to Write: A Book About Art, Independence and Spirit*. Saint Paul: Graywolf Press, 1938.

Section Two: *Nuts and Bolts*

These books address the hands-on job of writing. Whether you're buying a computer, or writing an outline for your first novel, or finding a writers' colony where you can finish your collection of short stories, these books can help. These are just a small selection of the many, many books out there designed to teach the "how-to" of writing. Some of them are very helpful. Some of them are not.

Bickman, Jack M. *Writing and Selling Your Novel*. Cincinnati, Ohio: Writer's Digest Books, 1996.

Block, Lawrence. *Writing the Novel: From Plot to Print*. Cincinnati, Ohio: Writer's Digest Books, 1979.

Bolker, Joan. *The Writer's Home Companion: An Anthology of the World's Best Writing Advice, from Keats to Kunitz*. New York: Henry Holt, 1997.

Bowler, Gail Hellund. *Artists & Writers Colonies: Retreats, Residencies, and Respites for the Creative Mind*. Hillsboro, Oregon: Blue Heron Publishing, 1995.

Browne, Renni, and Dave King. *Self-Editing for Writers: How to Edit Yourself into Print*. New York: HarperPerennial: A Division of HarperCollins Publishers, 1994.

Burnett, Hallie, and Whit. *Fiction Writer's Handbook*. New York: HarperPerennial: A Division of HarperCollins Publishers, 1975.

Burroway, Janet. *Writing Fiction: A Guide to Narrative Craft*. New York: Addison-Wesley, 1999.

Cameron, Julia. *The Artist's Way: A Spiritual Path to Higher Creativity*. New York: Putnam, 1992.

Cameron, Julia. *The Vein of Gold: A Journey to Your Creative Heart*. New York: G. P. Putnam's Sons, 1996.

Clark, Tom, William Brohaugh, et al., eds. *The Writer's Digest Handbook of Novel Writing*. Cincinnati, Ohio: Writer's Digest Books, 1992.

Collier, Oscar, and Frances Spatz Leighton. *How to Write & Sell Your First Novel*. Cincinnati, Ohio: Writer's Digest Books, 1997.

Edelstein, Scott. *The No-Experience-Necessary Writer's Course: A Unique Stress-Free Approach for Anyone Who Has Ever Wanted to Write*. Chelsea, Michigan: Scarborough House, 1990.

Edelstein, Scott. *30 Steps to Becoming a Writer and Getting Published: The Complete Starter Kit for Aspiring Writers*. Cincinnati, Ohio: Writer's Digest Books, 1993.

Edgar, Christopher, and Ron Padgett, eds. *Old Faithful: 18 Present Their Favorite Writing Assignments*. New York: Teachers & Writers Collaborative, 1995.

Frank, Thaisa, and Dorothy Wall. *Finding Your Writer's Voice: A Guide to Creative Fiction*. New York: St. Martin's Griffin, 1994.

Hills, Rust. *Writing in General and the Short Story in Particular*. Boston: Houghton Mifflin, 1977, 1987.

Keyes, Ralph. *The Courage to Write: How Writers Transcend Fear*. New York: Henry Holt, 1995.

Levin, Donna. *Get That Novel Started! (And Keep It Going 'Til You Finish): A Practical, Inspirational Guide for Getting the Novel Within You Underway, Including How to Find the Idea, Avoid Being Overwhelmed and Dive into the Writing*. Cincinnati, Ohio: Writer's Digest Books, 1992.

Levin, Donna. *Get That Novel Written!* Cincinnati, Ohio: Writer's Digest Books, 1996.

Neubauer, Alexander. *Conversations on Writing Fiction: Interviews with 13 Distinguished Teachers of Fiction Writing in America*. New York: HarperPerennial: A Division of HarperCollins Publishers, 1994.

Newman, Leslea. *Writing from the Heart: Inspiration and Exercises for Women Who Want to Write*. Freedom, California: The Crossing Press, 1993.

Olmstead, Robert. *Elements of the Writing Craft*. Cincinnati, Ohio: Story Press, 1997.

Ray, Robert J. *The Weekend Novelist*. New York: A Dell Trade Paperback, Dell, 1994.

Stein, Sol. *Stein on Writing: A Master Editor of the Most Successful Writers of Our Century Shares His Craft Techniques and Strategy*. New York: St. Martin's Press, 1995.

Vogler, Christopher. *The Writer's Journey: Mythic Structure for Storytellers & Screenwriters.* Studio City, California: A Michael Wiese Productions Book, 1992.

White, Myles. *How to Buy a Computer: Or Upgrade What You Have.* Toronto: McCelland & Stewart, 1996.

Section Three: *Writer Reference*

One of the many fun things about being a writer is this: Just about any book on any topic can be considered research. A study on the shoe styles of medieval women? Essential. A book on the mating behavior of dolphins? A must have. These are some basic research and reference books for the well-informed writer. (One personal favorite of mine is the *Visual Dictionary.* This fascinating book will come to your aid on those days when you just can't remember, for the life of you the word for that round metal doohickey that you open doors with . . .) No writer's library would be complete without some of the real basics—a good dictionary, a good thesaurus, Strunk & White, Bartletts, Nortons.

Atchity, Kenneth J., ed. *The Classical Greek Reader.* New York: Oxford University Press, 1996.

Barraclough, Geoffrey, Geoffrey Parker, eds. *The Times Atlas of World History,* 4th Edition. Union, New Jersey: Hammond, 1993.

Bartlett, John. *Familiar Quotations.* Boston: Little, Brown, annual.

Biedermann, Hans. *Dictionary of Symbolism: Cultural Icons & the Meanings Behind Them.* San Diego: A Meridian Book, 1992.

Boorstin, Daniel J. *The Creators: A History of Heroes of the Imagination.* New York: Vintage Books, 1993.

Boorstin, Daniel J. *The Discoverers: A History of Man's Search to Know His World and Himself.* New York: Random House, 1985.

Boorstin, Daniel J. *The Seekers: The Story of Man's Continuing Quest to Understand His World.* New York: Random House, 1998.

Campbell, Joseph (commentary). *The Complete Grimm's Fairy Tales.* New York: Pantheon Books, 1972.

Clark, Thomas, Bruce Woods, et al., eds. *The Writer's Digest: Guide to Good Writing.* Cincinnati, Ohio: Writer's Digest Books, 1994.

Craig, Patricia, ed. *The Oxford Book of Travel Stories.* Oxford and New York: Oxford University Press, 1996.

Dillard, Annie, and Cort Conley. *Modern American Memoirs*. New York: HarperCollins, 1995.

Donald, Roger, ed. *Bartlett's Roget's Thesaurus*. Boston: Little, Brown, 1996.

Fisher, David, and Reginald Bragonier Jr. *What's What: A Visual Glossary of the Physical World*. Maplewood, New Jersey: Hammond, 1990.

Garvey, Mark, ed. *Writer's Market: Where & How to Sell What You Write*. Cincinnati, Ohio: Writer's Digest Books, annual.

Grossman, John (preface). *The Chicago Manual of Style: The Essential Guide for Writers, Editors, and Publishers*, 14th edition. Chicago, Illinois: University of Chicago Press, 1993.

Hammond Atlas of the World. Union, New Jersey: Hammond, 1998.

Hirsch, E. D. Jr., Joseph F. Kett, and James Trefil. *The Dictionary of Cultural Literacy*. Boston: Houghton Mifflin, 1988.

Kuroff, Barbara, ed. *Novel & Short Story Writer's Market*. Cincinnati, Ohio: Writer's Digest Books, annual.

The Macmillan Visual Dictionary. New York: Macmillan, 1992.

Maltin, Leonard. *Movie & Video Guide*. New York: A Plume Book, annual.

Merriam-Webster's Collegiate Dictionary, 10th edition. Springfield, Massachusetts: Merriam-Webster, 1993.

Owens, Lily, ed. *The Complete Hans Christian Andersen Fairy Tales: Little Known Tales as Well as Treasured Classics*. New York: Avenel Books, 1984.

Philip, George. *Oxford Atlas of the World*. New York: Oxford University Press, 1998.

Robinson, Andrew. *The Story of Writing*. New York: Thames and Hudson, 1995.

Shakespeare, William. *The Complete Signet Classic Shakespeare*. New York: Harcourt Brace Jovanovich, 1972.

Skeat, Walter W. *The Concise Dictionary of English Etymology*. New York: Wordsworth Reference, 1993.

Stilman, Anne. *Grammatically Correct: The Writer's Essential Guide to Punctuation, Spelling, Style, Usage and Grammar*. Cincinnati, Ohio: Writer's Digest Books, 1997.

Strunk, William & E. B. White. *Elements of Style*. Needham Heights, Massachusetts: Allyn & Bacon, 1995.

Wallechinsky, David. *The 20th Century: The Definitive Compendium of Astonishing Events, Amazing People, and Strange-But-True Facts*. Boston: Little, Brown, 1995.

Section Four: *The Big Picture*

I thought it would be good to include a few books that ask the bigger picture: specifically, "What Does It *Mean* to Be an Artist?" While these might not be directed at the writer in the crowd, the existential questions they pose can stimulate and challenge the mind, and the heart, of any artist. If you have time to read, or reread, any of these, you will find yourself looking at your work and your life with fresh, inquisitive eyes.

Fadiman, Clifton, and John S. Major. *The New Lifetime Reading Plan.* New York: HarperCollins, 1997.

Lévi-Strauss, Claude. *Look, Listen, Read.* New York: Basic Books: A Member of the Perseus Books Club, 1997.

Pinker, Steven. *The Language Instinct: How the Mind Creates Language.* New York: HarperPerennial, 1994.

Rostenberg, Leona, and Madeleine Stern. *Old Books, Rare Friends: Two Literary Sleuths and Their Shared Passion.* New York: Main Street Books, Doubleday, 1997.

Sarton, May. *Journal of a Solitude.* New York and London: W. W. Norton, 1973.

Woolf, Virginia. *A Room of One's Own.* San Diego: Harcourt Brace, 1929.

About the Author

Caroline Sharp has a degree in psychology from Princeton University and an MFA from Columbia University. She has also completed the Writer's Boot Camp and Think Tank programs in Los Angeles. She lives with her husband, two children, and a puppy in New York City, where she is at work on a novel.